Continuous Improvement in High Schools

Continuous Improvement in High Schools

Helping More Students Succeed

Martha Abele Mac Iver
Robert Balfanz

HARVARD EDUCATION PRESS
CAMBRIDGE, MASSACHUSETTS

Paperback ISBN 978-1-68253-685-8

Library of Congress Cataloging-in-Publication data is on file.

Published by Harvard Education Press,
an imprint of the Harvard Education Publishing Group

Harvard Education Press
8 Story Street
Cambridge, MA 02138

Cover Design: Endpaper Studio
Cover Photo: shuoshu/DigitalVision Vectors via Getty Images

The typefaces used in this book are Sabon and ITC Legacy Sans.

To the high school students across
the United States, together with their teachers
and all the other educators who serve them.
You have inspired our work and this book.

Contents

Introduction

The importance of a high school diploma has never been clearer. It is no longer an end point on the road to adult success but an essential stepping stone to postsecondary schooling or training.[1] This has led to federal, state, and local efforts to both raise high school graduation rates and align high school graduation requirements with postsecondary readiness.[2] Over the past two decades these efforts to raise high school graduation rates have been a considerable success. In 2003 the high school graduation rate stood at about 74 percent—just about where it had been for the prior thirty years.[3] In 2018, the most recent year of available data, the US high school graduation rate had increased to 85 percent, an increase of 11 percentage points over fifteen years.[4] Although minority and low-income students remain less likely than white students to graduate, the increase in graduation rates has been largely driven by improved outcomes for these historically underserved groups.

Closer analysis of the progress in raising graduation rates reveals that while all states and subgroups of students have shown some improvement, the rate of improvement has been uneven, and some districts show little if any progress. The progress achieved was not primarily driven by large structural changes which raised graduation rates for everyone. Rather, improvement resulted when schools, districts, and states—in part spurred on by graduation rate accountability—worked the problem. Those that stuck with it and worked the problem the longest saw the greatest sustained gains over time.[5]

Even with these improvements, as the second decade of the twenty-first century came to a close, there remained significant groups of students with low graduation rates. These groups included students with disabilities and English language learners; students in states with very large graduation gaps between middle- and upper-income white students and low-income students of color; and many students who attended the over two thousand regular, alternative, charter, and virtual high schools with graduation rates below 67 percent.[6]

Then came March 2020's Friday the 13th—the last day of in-person classes for much of the nation as COVID-19 began to ravage the globe. What seemed to be a short extension of spring break grew into more than a year of interrupted learning opportunities as hospitals filled to the breaking point in the spring of 2020, and cases surged once again after Thanksgiving. Schools scrambled to implement online learning solutions, while those without internet access or the devices they needed to participate in virtual classrooms were left behind. Even those who could theoretically access the technology needed for this new learning environment were likely to disengage. Projections suggest there will be significant learning loss and widening achievement gaps between historically underserved students and others.[7]

How will we be able to sustain and improve upon the increased high school graduation rates of the past fifteen years as we move into the post–COVID-19 recovery period? In particular, given what we can expect about student learning loss and the disengagement students experienced during virtual learning in the pandemic, particularly in the secondary grades, how will high schools be able to improve the ninth grade outcomes that have been shown to be the leading indicators of on-time postsecondary-ready high school graduation? As most students were forced to learn virtually during Fall 2020, there was evidence of widespread course failure at higher rates than seen in the past.[8] This does not bode well for improving, or even maintaining, high school graduation rates.

We are not without recourse. We have learned much in the past two decades on how to improve high school graduation and post-secondary readiness rates. New tools and approaches are being developed to enable schools to localize and customize this knowledge to their particular circumstances and, in many cases, to create their own powerful solutions. In this book we utilize the continuous improvement framework that has emerged as a powerful way to investigate, test out, and identify effective solutions to problems like chronic absence and course failure that are so closely linked to high school success.[9] We draw on our deep knowledge of the challenges faced by high schools and our decades of experience working with educators to guide readers as they seek to push into the knowledge frontier and apply a continuous improvement framework to student success in high school, starting with the critical ninth grade year.

WHY IS NINTH GRADE SO CRITICAL?

Over the past two decades the research we and others have conducted has shown that the first year of high school is a "make or break year."[10] As students make the transition to high school they find learning environments less supportive than those in elementary and middle schools. While most upper-grade elementary students report their teachers regularly recognize them for good work, few ninth graders do.[11] Ninth graders are frequently unprepared to navigate this new environment where teachers give zeros for missed assignments and courses must be passed to earn the credits required for graduation and often grade promotion. They encounter many teachers who believe that it is up to students to learn how to succeed in high school and that experiencing the consequences for not being responsible is an important life lesson. Some, experiencing greater independence for the first time, believe they can skip some school and blow off a few assignments and make it up later, only to learn too late that the zeros have added up and it will be hard to pass no matter what they do. Others find themselves afraid to ask for help before it is too late to avoid a failing grade, or they start missing school because they are being bullied or do not feel safe.

Research findings have confirmed not only the strong association between absence and failing grades, but also the critical role of ninth grade failure in the probability of on-time high school graduation. A student's grade point average (GPA) in ninth grade has been shown to be a key predictor of later high school outcomes and postsecondary enrollment and success rates.[12] Ninth grade failure has lasting effects.[13] Once students fall behind in earning credits needed for graduation, it is difficult to catch up. Getting back on track is not impossible, but it takes the concerted efforts of adults to help students recover from the consequences of early failure. Students often experience a downward spiral from their experiences of high-stakes failure and need intervention to turn things around. Although this seems intuitively obvious, in the years before these research findings became widely known schools were not particularly well-organized to intervene as ninth graders began falling off track. As a high school dropout told Michelle Fine several decades ago:

> Teachers never paid no attention to me. I didn't like school or the teachers, and so I cut out . . . [When] I made an effort to get to school on time . . . I still failed. So I said I have to stop going. I'm not getting anywhere. Just keep getting left behind.[14]

Hundreds of thousands of students from that era could echo this story.

Now that the research findings about the impact of ninth grade failure have been widely disseminated, more districts and high schools are paying attention to ninth grade outcomes and setting goals for ninth grade credit accumulation.[15] But challenges remain for schools in actually attaining these goals. What is needed to improve ninth grade student outcomes? What do schools need to do to ensure that students are attending regularly, engaged in schooling, achieving learning goals, and producing the academic work needed for them to earn their course credits?

WHY IS CONTINUOUS IMPROVEMENT A PROMISING APPROACH?

Over the past decade policymakers and educational researchers have recognized the value of a continuous improvement framework, also called improvement science, for addressing educational problems.[16] There are a growing number of such frameworks educators can draw on. Among them, the Carnegie Foundation's framework is a promising approach for making progress in helping more students complete high school prepared for the postsecondary training they will need for the twenty-first-century workplace.[17]

First, it provides a systematic structure for educators and their collaborating partners to examine the root causes of the problems they are seeking to address. Rather than simply trying to apply a solution to the problem before they fully understand it, educators become equipped to address the underlying issues that produce or contribute to the problems they face in getting all students to earn a high school diploma with the skills to succeed in postsecondary education.

Second, the continuous improvement framework focuses the attention of educators on the system within which their particular problems are nested and teaches them how to "see the system that produces the problem."[18] If we are to solve the complex problems we face, we need more people who have been trained to think about systems and how they interact to influence the particular issues we confront.

Third, the framework provides a systematic way to test ideas and draw conclusions based on data analysis about how well they are working in the context in which they need to succeed. Using the framework keeps us focused on ensuring we are following through on collecting and analyzing data about how well a particular change or intervention is working (something that often falls through the cracks in most schools we have observed). It also helps avoid the all too common pitfall of importing a solution without establishing that a school's and district's local circumstances can enable its desired outcomes.

Fourth, the Carnegie Foundation's approach to continuous improvement emphasizes the importance of building networked learning communities of teams who are working on similar problems across multiple sites. Building such networks to facilitate shared learning can potentially help us to solve education problems more quickly.

OUR LEARNING JOURNEY

In this book we share some conclusions we have drawn from what we have learned in our continuous improvement journey. We still have much to learn ourselves, but were encouraged to pass on what we have seen thus far about applying a continuous improvement framework to our work. Over the past twenty-five years we have worked in multiple ways with schools and districts across the country to try to improve high school (and particularly ninth grade) student outcomes.

Bob Balfanz's work on *Everyday Mathematics* and *Big Math for Little Kids* at the University of Chicago attracted the attention of the Johns Hopkins Center for Social Organization of Schools (CSOS) in the mid-1990s, and they invited him to dive into the work of transforming the lowest performing high schools in Baltimore and middle-grade schools in Philadelphia. The high school goal was to help scale the new Talent Development High School model to more high-poverty neighborhood high schools.[19] Central to the model was dividing large comprehensive high schools into a separate ninth grade academy and multiple tenth to twelfth grade career academies. The ninth grade academy used teams of teachers who shared common sets of students to combat the anonymity that students reported as a contributor to their disengagement, while helping them to close skill and knowledge gaps and attend school regularly to enable them to earn on-time promotion to tenth grade.

Together with CSOS colleagues, Bob spent hundreds of hours within the high schools, gaining deep understanding of what it took to transform them into productive learning communities. Spending significant time in the schools with which he was working to develop reforms was not only essential to successful implementation, but also provided most of the insights that led to later research findings. As he and his colleagues worked to help more schools implement the Talent Development school reform model, they noticed a common pattern: there would be wild and impassioned graduation ceremonies that typically involved a little over one hundred students, but these same schools had about four hundred ninth graders. Often there were as many ninth graders in the hallways as in the classrooms.

This led Bob and his colleague, Nettie Legters, to wonder how common the pyramid of many ninth graders and few twelfth graders really was. Their widely influential report on *Locating the Dropout Crisis* documented the existence of about two thousand "dropout factory" high schools where the senior class could be as much as 60 percent smaller than the freshman class.[20] These findings, together with research indicating that much better outcomes could be achieved in these schools by applying comprehensive reform models like Talent Development, helped provide an impetus for broader national efforts to reform these schools and establish accountability measures for high school graduation rates.

Through Bob's vision and efforts, the Talent Development model evolved into Diplomas Now, which combined the whole-school reform model with enhanced student supports (provided by City Year and Communities in Schools) as well as with an early warning and intervention system (another CSOS model and tool). Although the adult capacity-building focus of the Talent Development models could help struggling schools improve considerably, too many students were still being left behind. The early warning indicator research led by Bob and colleagues showed that in high-poverty secondary schools there were often hundreds of students who were struggling to attend every day, focus in class, behave in school, and get their assignments done.[21] It was clear that more person power was needed in these schools to meet the scale and intensity levels of students' needs. And an early warning system was necessary to help get the right supports to the right students at the right time. The model went through a rapid prototype and design phase, and with funding from the US Department of Education Investing in Innovation (i3) program, it showed positive results in a large national randomized field trial. Findings indicated that Diplomas Now helped to increase the number of students who ended the sixth grade with no early warning indicators in attendance, behavior, and course failure.[22]

Bob continues his efforts to help schools and districts improve learning opportunities and outcomes for students through the work of the CSOS Everyone Graduates Center (EGC) with the Compass Academy in Denver, the New Mexico Early Warning Systems partnership, the Cross State High School Redesign Collaborative, and the Pathways to Adult Success learning community, among other initiatives.[23] Currently he is helping organize and support a Gates Foundation–funded Networks for School Improvement project focused on improving eighth grade on-track outcomes within high-poverty middle schools in multiple districts. He is also leading a large study of the implementation of a social-emotional learning curriculum for eighth grade students to prepare them for the transition to high school. And as he describes the work of our research and development center at Johns Hopkins, "We always have one model in the field, one in the shop, and one in our heads."[24]

Martha made the transition from political science to education research after nearly two decades of studying the Northern Ireland conflict and the transition to democracy in eastern Europe after the fall of the Berlin Wall. Since the mid-1990s she has spent many hours observing in schools across the K–12 spectrum—shadowing students, observing classroom instruction, conducting focus groups with students and teachers, and seeking to understand the impact of multiple interventions on student outcomes. Since the mid-2000s she has partnered with district leaders in several studies, conducting longitudinal data analysis to understand the impact of various factors on student outcomes and helping district and school staff to implement promising practices to improve student outcomes. Her research with others at the Everyone Graduates Center in district after district found the same patterns and conclusions about the importance of ninth grade performance on high school graduation outcomes.[25] She collaborated on a large-scale study of implementing early warning and intervention systems in twenty high schools in the effort to improve ninth grade attendance and course passing rates. In another recent project she worked with a team of researchers and educators to develop and pilot a professional development series for high school teachers focused on helping them to change instructional and assessment practices in ways that would increase student engagement with learning. This entailed working with teachers at three different high schools over three years to engage them in interactive professional development and elicit their feedback on how to make the sessions more engaging and effective. Another recent four-year partnership with one district followed a continuous improvement approach in seeking to equip middle and high school staff to more effectively engage families during the high school transition, with the aim of improving ninth grade student attendance and course performance. Over the four years of the project her team learned from regular meetings and professional development sessions with leaders or teams from more than twenty schools, as well as from observation of more than two dozen family engagement events. This approach of deep engagement with practitioners—as we work together in research and development to improve education for historically underserved students—has characterized the work of EGC for many decades.

In recent years we both have been seeking to follow a continuous improvement approach to the problem of low rates of college- and career-ready high school graduation. This work has built on our analysis of ninth grade course failure and middle school early warning indicators in attendance, behavior, and course failure, which are leading indicators of negative high school outcomes. While high school graduation rates have risen considerably over the past two decades, considerable gaps remain between students of different ethnicities and socioeconomic groups. Ensuring that all students graduate from high school—and are prepared for postsecondary education to support their readiness for the twenty-first-century workplace—is one of the country's most important educational priorities. It is imperative to provide the kind of educational experiences in every classroom that will engage all students' hearts and minds and equip them with the skills for effective communication, problem-solving, and collaborative, productive teamwork. We believe it is possible to create the kinds of high schools where students from historically underserved communities throughout our country can engage in joyful collaborative learning about how to solve problems they care about deeply. We know they can succeed in demonstrating their abilities to communicate effectively in well-crafted podcasts, multimedia presentations, and editorials about the underlying causes of community problems and potential solutions for them. They can engage in stimulating scientific and social research and present their findings effectively and creatively. We need to create the conditions in which they can flourish. This book considers some of the practical steps that can lead to improvement in high school students' educational experiences and outcomes.

OVERVIEW OF THE BOOK

In this book we seek to model a way of applying the continuous improvement framework from the Carnegie Foundation for the Advancement of Teaching to the specific issue of improving high school outcomes. We organize the book around the six improvement principles outlined in *Learning to Improve: How America's Schools Can Get Better at Getting Better*:[26]

- Make the work problem-specific and user-centered
- Focus on variation in performance
- See the system that produces the current outcomes
- Emphasize measurement to "improve at scale"
- Use disciplined inquiry to drive improvement
- Accelerate learning through networked communities

In each of the following chapters we provide some specific examples of how these principles can be fleshed out in the context of improving outcomes for high school students in the United States. The book aims to be a practical guide to teams of educators seeking to apply a continuous improvement framework to solving the specific problem of too many students who are failing to complete high school prepared for the postsecondary education needed for economic survival in the twenty-first century.

In particular, we will focus on several broad umbrellas of changes that research suggests are promising levers for improving high school outcomes. These five umbrellas are:

- early warning and intervention systems;
- engaging families to support ninth grade students;
- increasing students' sense of connectedness to school;
- accelerating and integrating student's social, emotional, and academic development; and
- transforming teacher instructional practices to motivate and engage students more deeply in academic work.

Based on our extensive experience working under each of these umbrellas, we will use specific examples of possible change ideas as we provide practical guidance in seeing the system, identifying root causes and improvement drivers, using practical measures for improvement, conducting disciplined inquiry, and accelerating learning through networked communities. This practical guide seeks to provide a roadmap and toolbox to help educators and policymakers in their own continuous improvement efforts around high school outcomes.

CHAPTER 1

Identifying the Problems and Consulting the Stakeholders

This first principle of improvement science in education addresses a general problem in educational practice and research—what Bryk and his colleagues call "solutionitis."[1] Many educational interventions have been developed by researchers or central office administrators based on their general education knowledge or understanding of "how things work" or "what is needed" based on their prior experiences and learnings. This can lead them to jump to solutions before completely understanding the specific problems schools are facing and their local context. Under time pressure, schools also often reach for solutions that are easily available without delving more deeply into the actual causes of problems so they can craft and fit solutions to address their specific challenges.

In this chapter we recommend three main strategies for avoiding "solutionitis" as educational leaders work to improve high school outcomes. These strategies emerge from our experience in seeking to apply the Carnegie Foundation's continuous improvement framework during our work with districts and schools across the country. We urge education leaders to use reliable research findings to guide the development of "carefully-defined, specific problem statements," to bring stakeholder/user groups together to be informed by varying perspectives, and to build consensus within district leadership and school stakeholders around broad improvement goals related to the identified problem.[2] Later chapters will dig more deeply into the process of identifying reasons for the problem and potential changes that could lead to improvements.

USE RELIABLE RESEARCH TO DEVELOP SPECIFIC PROBLEM STATEMENTS

Finding the right balance between leveraging the knowledge of primary stakeholders (school personnel, students, and families) and building on prior research is part of the art of continuous improvement. In our experience, where we place the fulcrum between these depends on the stage of the improvement work and the levels of reliable research evidence available. Given the time constraints education practitioners operate under, we recommend following the advice given in a recent Carnegie Foundation blog to give stakeholders a "carefully-defined, specific problem statement."[3] This does not prevent the stakeholders from weighing in on the definition of the problem as they identify and discuss root causes. But it prevents the kind of extended debate over selecting and defining problems that can devour the time available for stakeholders to spend on the continuous improvement process. While at times it may be useful to spend months on problem definition, it is generally more important to steward that time for the user-centered discussions that can lead to progress in understanding causes and identifying potential change ideas.

Improving high school graduation rates became a common metric on district strategic plans once the National Governor's Association and other policy leaders had succeeded in making the need to improve high school graduation rates a national priority.[4] But it has taken a while for district leaders to begin paying attention to the converging national research on specific leading indicators associated with high school graduation. While it seems obvious that ninth grade course passing (credit accumulation) is strongly correlated with total credit accumulation in twelfth grade and the probability of meeting all the requirements for high school graduation, our early experience with numerous districts uncovered a reticence in many places to focus specifically on ninth grade failure. Even when districts have a stated goal of ensuring that all students graduate prepared for college, career, and life and include "ninth graders earning sufficient credits" as a metric on their school reports, they have not necessarily identified high rates of ninth grade failure as a problem that needs to be addressed. As we noted in the Introduction, research in dozens of districts across the country has identified the important relationship between ninth grade course passing and graduation outcomes, as well as the close association between attendance and course passing. Researchers in Chicago have demonstrated that systematic monitoring and intervention in ninth grade has led to improved high school graduation rates in that district.[5]

Based on that research, it makes sense for district and school leaders to examine their own patterns of ninth grade course passing outcomes (as we discuss in more detail in chapter 2). District level analyses may also identify earlier issues, such as middle school chronic absenteeism or gaps in student learning, that need to be addressed in a holistic, systemic approach to improving high school outcomes. But it is essential to take a critical look at areas like ninth grade failure that have already been identified by national research, and to identify these failure rates as a problem to solve (rather than simply a fact of life to be tolerated or even expected).

GATHER PERSPECTIVES AND INSIGHTS FROM STAKEHOLDERS AT MULTIPLE LEVELS

Being user-centered means listening to those who are closest to the work. In this section we consider several dimensions of that process. First, we discuss the importance of bringing together the different district or management organization leaders who own pieces of the work and facilitating regular and active communication within this team. Second, we consider the process of gathering perspectives from multiple stakeholders at the school level (including principals, teachers, students, and families). Third, we emphasize the need to expect divergent views and philosophies and be prepared to negotiate conflict.

Build a Cross-Functional District Team Focused on the Problem

Improving high school outcomes requires focused attention from a team of district leaders.[6] Who needs to be on such a team? We would argue that representation from several functional roles is critical. Those who supervise high school principals are essential. When districts are organized only geographically and supervision of high school principals is fragmented among many individuals who are focused on much more than high schools, this could be challenging. Larger districts need a leader focused on high schools who at least shares some authority over the work of high school principals. A college and career readiness director role is critical for such a team, but these leaders may not have the needed influence over high school principals. We would argue that such a team should also include district leaders focused on research and accountability, given the importance of using data in the continuous improvement process (discussed more fully in later chapters). Because teachers and families are also important stakeholders, it is important to include leaders focused on high school teacher professional development and family engagement. This team would ideally report to a high-ranking district leader as it considers and addresses how to increase successful high school outcomes.

Gather Perspectives from Multiple Stakeholders at the School Level

As it addresses the problem of ninth grade failure, the cross-functional district team should be encouraged to convene separate listening sessions with high school principals, teachers and other staff members, students, and family members. (A school leadership team could do the same thing with the school community groups listed above.) At a later stage, such sessions could focus more on generating ideas about root causes and potential changes that could drive improvement, and it might even be possible to begin such discussions at a first meeting. But the primary goal of first meetings with stakeholders is to assess the degree of consensus around the importance of the problem and the willingness of stakeholders to engage in improvement efforts. We would recommend sharing research findings and data with stakeholder groups in appropriate ways (discussed in more detail in chapter 2). One could even frame such meetings as "listening sessions" to gather opinions from the various groups about how important the issue of ninth grade student credit accumulation is for the local education community to address. Ideally the district team could convene listening sessions with each of the four different groups (principals, teachers and staff, families, and students) over the course of a month or two. If possible, it would be useful to have separate meetings at several different high schools with teachers and staff, students, and families. The team should plan to collect detailed notes (and recordings if possible) and analyze the comments from stakeholders for common themes and divergent viewpoints.

Expect Divergent Views and Philosophies

One of the things we have learned in discussions with multiple stakeholders over many years is that the issue of high school grading and failure evokes deep emotion and sharp divisions between people who hold conflicting views. Often these divisions influence leaders to avoid inevitably conflictual discussions. But top-down decision-making around grading and failure prevention often results in backlash from disgruntled stakeholders.[7] We believe it is important to engage in conversations around these issues with some prior preparation to help stakeholders reflect on their beliefs and be willing to consider other viewpoints.

Some people wholeheartedly believe that failure is a good learning experience and that the idea of working to reduce high school course failure through prevention efforts is completely misguided. They cite the experience of entrepreneurs who embrace failure as the route to success. Echoing Paul Tough, they ask, "What if the key to success is failure?"[8] Elsewhere we have argued that dialogue with those who hold these views should include questions about the differences between failure in universally necessary life tasks (like learning to read and completing a K–12 education in twenty-first-century American society) and the more optional tasks at which not everyone can or will succeed (like making the team or being admitted to a selective college).[9] Failing at high-stakes and universally necessary tasks like earning the credits necessary for graduating from high school is not the same kind of "productive failure" as failing to make a sports team. It is also important to point out how course failure is not distributed randomly; it affects certain demographic groups much more than others, often because students whose parents have the information and connections to be effective advocates are generally sheltered from the failure outcomes that less advantaged students face. When historically underserved students receive the message from report cards that they are failures, it often leads to a downward spiral rather than the kind of resilience touted by entrepreneurs.[10]

Other education practitioners we have encountered over the past decades voice concerns that any efforts to reduce failure will effectively lead to lower academic rigor. Some even believe that a certain percentage of students should be expected to fail as evidence that academic expectations are sufficiently rigorous. One can understand this mindset among college instructors whom we trust to determine which students may not have the prerequisite knowledge to succeed in such fields as medicine and engineering. Some types of failure are probably necessary. The question we need to help people consider is how we should think about failure to achieve basic skills and credentials needed for basic levels of economic survival in society. To what extent is such failure due to systemic issues? We consider this more fully in chapter 3.

Another prominent theme in discussions of high school course failure is the need to teach students responsibility and the work ethic.

Teacher objections to grading systems that help students to recover from early failure reflect the view that such practices do not prepare them for the real world workforce. One teacher we overheard during a professional development session on assessment practices even mentioned O-rings and the Challenger disaster as an example of times in the real world that you only get one chance to get it right. These same teachers do not appear to object to giving students the opportunity to retake entire courses in summer school or the following year—but they do not believe in building recovery opportunities into courses the first time. Again, some amiable dialogue may be in order. They may have forgotten that their own supervisors do not just give them zeroes when they do not submit a report on time—they are still expected to submit the work. Continued patterns of missed deadlines and uncompleted assignments in the workplace trigger interventions such as progressive counseling that can often (though admittedly not always) turn things around.

Many teachers continue to affirm their autonomy in the grading process and their unilateral right to assign failing course grades. This right has even been tested in first amendment cases in the courts.[11] Dialogue around this issue is often contentious. Is it possible to engage in civil discourse around the pros and cons of common grading systems designed to promote equity and fairness?

There tends to be more support among stakeholders for interventions that could reduce failure rates by encouraging greater monitoring of student grades and providing tutoring for students to improve their performance. But there may be disagreements over allocation of scarce resources when such interventions compete with other educational programs that benefit students who are not struggling to pass their courses. Achieving agreement around the issue of course failure can certainly be a challenge.

BUILD CONSENSUS ON IMPROVEMENT GOALS TO ADDRESS THE PROBLEM

The endpoint of this process of facilitating stakeholder discussion is to collaboratively build consensus on overarching improvement goals to address the problem. The examples of divergent views on high school failure described above may give us pause about whether it is actually possible to achieve consensus.

One way to facilitate consensus building is to help stakeholders "begin with the end in mind," as Stephen Covey has put it.[12] If the goal of K–12 education is to successfully launch students into the workplace and/or further preparation for a career, what steps do we need to take to get there? If ninth grade academic outcomes are a key indicator of later high school success, how do we go about improving those outcomes? Why would we be afraid of setting a goal to reduce the failure rate in ninth grade? Can we agree that increasing success in the critical ninth grade year can help us reach the goal we all agree on—increasing the proportion of students who leave high school prepared for a career and/or postsecondary education?

The process of consensus building may also move forward when we recognize (as we discuss in more detail in the following chapter) that the students we are trying to move from failure to success in ninth grade are disproportionately students of color or from low-income households who have been historically underserved. A focus on issues of equity and justice can potentially facilitate the process. It may be possible to mobilize support by framing the goal as improving ninth grade on-track credit accumulation for students of color who historically have not experienced equitable educational opportunities. Research has shown considerable evidence of teachers' racial bias in student evaluation.[13] Recognizing this problem of ninth grade failure as an equity issue that requires focused attention is a critical step in the continuous improvement process.

LISTEN TO STUDENTS—THE PRIMARY STAKEHOLDERS

As we seek to build consensus on improvement goals we cannot emphasize enough the importance of listening to the stakeholders most invested in high school outcomes. And the primary stakeholders—those with the most vested interest—are really the students themselves. We frankly do not spend enough time listening to the voices of students and their families. Our colleague, Richard Lofton, makes a compelling case for redressing this glaring oversight in his "Nobody Asked Me" campaign and research study in Baltimore.[14] When we listen to the voices of students we can begin to understand their experiences of school. For many historically underserved students in urban communities, school is not a welcoming place. As one young adult in one of Lofton's studies described her school experience:

> You're constantly yelled at. Constantly punished. Constantly hear doors slamming through the day. Books being thrown. Teachers at their wits' end. It's not a positive environment to learn.[15]

Sitting through some classroom instruction is so excruciatingly dull that incentives for attendance are simply not worth it. Much of what goes on in school does not seem relevant to students' lives. It is not surprising that many simply vote with their feet and decide not to go.

It doesn't have to be this way. School faculty and staff can and must build positive, nurturing relationships with students. And when students experience great instruction through methods such as project-based learning that relate to their lives, they are enthusiastic about their academic work at school. As one student described her experience with project-based learning:

> You think . . . it's going to get boring. We never get bored. We look at it [the topic we're studying] in so many different ways. . . . So when it comes down to Exhibition class, people are just so stunned with all the work we did and it makes us feel so much better about ourselves because we've learned so much.[16]

Another student summarized her experience with project-based learning this way: "It really, actually changed my life and how I look at things."[17]

When we really listen to the primary stakeholders, we begin to understand the problems in ways that can generate promising change ideas. Listening to student voices can't just be an occasional activity. It needs to be built into our organizational routines within schools and districts. It will be well worth the effort. Students themselves often come up with the best ideas.

CHAPTER 2

Examining the Variation in High School Outcomes and Inputs

Variation is a wonderful thing in jazz. We value variation in nature and all the art forms. But we do begin to worry about variation in the quality of our health-care experiences. And we need to consider variation in educational experience and outcomes more closely, because certain types of variation are toxic rather than wonderful. If we are seeking to improve outcomes for all children, we need to pay attention to this variation and figure out why it occurs. Analyzing this variation helps us to uncover some of the factors related to it—what factors are present in cases of high performance that are not present in cases of low performance. When we begin to understand these factors and how they are related to performance, we can begin to specify some "standard work processes" in education that need attention.[1]

Researchers have shined a spotlight on this variation in educational experience for several decades. As one research team vividly described the educational situation in the 1990s:

> Depending on which school a child attends and to which classrooms the child is assigned, the student will encounter a varied array of programs and activities. . . . From the students' perspective, then, the quality of their educational experiences rests on the "luck of the draw."[2]

These researchers concluded that it was the responsibility of the central school district office leadership to "remove this luck factor from the instructional program, i.e., to ensure that idiosyncratic variations in programs, people, and policies do not result in systematic differences in the quality of education for children."[3] This variation does not just characterize classroom curricular programs or the availability of rigorous courses. Understanding the variation in important measures like high school graduation rates and ninth grade course failure rates is crucial in any attempt to pursue improved outcomes and improvements in the processes that influence them.

In this chapter we make some recommendations of how education practitioners can apply this principle of attending to variation in performance. We focus particularly on the process of examining variation in high school (particularly ninth grade) outcomes. As we mentioned in chapter 1, sharing findings from data analysis about variation across different groups within the system can be an important part of discussions with stakeholders as one seeks to "make the work problem-specific and user-centered."[4] Following the six improvement principles does not necessarily occur in a linear order—sometimes the dimensions are woven together. We offer specific recommendations below about how education practitioners can themselves (or in partnership with outside researchers) focus on variation in performance by analyzing outcome data in multiple ways and collecting and analyzing input data and its relationship to outcomes.

ANALYZE OUTCOME DATA IN MULTIPLE WAYS

Understanding patterns in the relevant data is a critical step in the continuous improvement process. One can begin with analyzing trends in aggregate high school outcome data (e.g., graduation rates, college enrollment rates, etc.), but it is very useful to delve more deeply in the analytical process. In the section below we describe an analytical process we have found helpful as we have worked with many different districts for more than a decade.

Building a longitudinal dataset that includes data from a cohort of ninth grade students over four years of high school is probably the best way to begin examining the variation in high school outcomes. The most critical variables to include are detailed information about the ninth grade record (attendance, course grades, disciplinary data if relevant, data on eligibility for/participation in special services, and demographic data). These same data from eighth grade, particularly attendance, are also useful if possible to include. Details about progression in grade level and withdrawal status over the four years (including graduation status at the end of the fourth year) are critical variables to include. While data on attendance and course grades in years after ninth grade can be useful, they are not essential for the proposed analyses. Building this dataset is not a heavy lift for most larger district research offices. Given the need to balance the task with other priorities it might take a month or two, but can be done relatively quickly if analytical resources are available. It is likely that nearby university researchers would gladly partner on such a task if the district is willing to form such a partnership.

Once analysts have defined the final outcome for each student in the cohort dataset after four years (graduated, still enrolled but not graduated, transferred to another school, dropped out, or unknown outcome), they can use the data to examine the relationship between demographic variables and the graduation (or nongraduation) outcome. Although the relationships can vary somewhat from place to place, analyses in dozens of districts find lower probability of graduation for males, students of color, special education students, and English language learners.[5] While demographic variables are important, it is essential to examine the more behavioral indicators of lower graduation rate probabilities that are actually malleable. What we found in district after district was that these demographic factors were often themselves associated with behaviors such as chronic absence and ninth grade course failure, and to a lesser extent with suspensions. The impact of demographic variables on graduation rates often becomes insignificant once analyses control for these behavioral indicators. In early studies these behavioral indicators were much more important than test scores in predicting the probability of graduation. When graduation requirements began to include a passing score on state graduation tests, those test scores become somewhat stronger predictors (though generally never as strong as ninth grade course failure). Recent research has also found that high school GPA is a better predictor of college completion than college entrance exams are.[6] High school grades matter a lot.

Even with more than a decade of similar findings, some districts still prefer to conduct their own ninth grade cohort study to examine the factors associated with failure to graduate on time from high school. Data from one's own district may carry more weight in discussions with stakeholders (even when the graphs look exactly the same as those from other districts). We include in figure 2.1 an example of findings from a study we conducted recently with a partner district. The graph looks almost identical to those from dozens of districts across the country. The percentage of students graduating on time from high school declines steadily for each core course failure in ninth grade.

FIGURE 2.1 Percentage of students graduating on time, by number of 9th grade core course failures

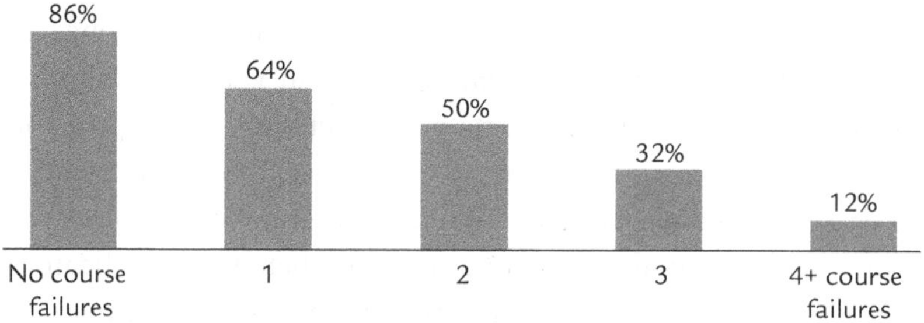

It is theoretically possible that you will not find a strong relationship between passing ninth grade courses and the probability of on-time graduation in your district. But it is highly unlikely. If you find the expected relationship, it is then important to analyze the variation in ninth grade failure rates. It is likely these analyses will reveal a similar pattern of relationships with demographic variables as the ones described above. But it is also important to analyze the relationship between ninth grade failure and other behavioral indicators, such as attendance. We have indeed found variation between districts and schools in the strength of the relationship between absenteeism and course failure. One should not jump to the conclusion, for example, that the 30 percent of students who are chronically absent are the same students as the 30 percent who fail at least one course. There can be varying degrees of overlap between these groups. Determining why students who attend regularly are still failing requires particular attention.

It is important for districts to examine the variation among high schools in rates of ninth grade failure, though some of the variation may be found to be attributable to differences in incoming student characteristics. For example, schools with selective admissions poli cies would be expected to have lower ninth grade failure rates. Non-selective schools can still have very different proportions of incoming students with prior records of chronic absence, which is a strong predictor of ninth grade failure. It is also possible that districts could identify variation between schools that needs further investigation to understand its causes. We discuss this in more detail in the section on input data below.

Analyses that explore the variation in ninth grade failure rates within schools by subject area, teacher, and class period can also be very useful in understanding the factors driving failure and how they might be addressed. For example, analyses by one district with which we partnered found an uptick in ninth grade science class failures after the adoption of a new curriculum. Another district we worked with identified a particular problem in algebra, with course grades driven almost completely by test scores. Further analyses indicated that these test scores were driven primarily by entering student skill levels that were attributable to prior years' instruction. In schools with tardiness issues, failure in first period classes is sometimes disproportionately higher than in classes later in the day. Higher rates of failure in courses taught by particular teachers could signal the use of particular practices (assigning zeros for uncompleted daily work, for example) that are associated with increased course failure rates. It is also possible that certain classrooms have disproportionately high numbers of students who need additional supports that have not been provided (such as recent immigrant students or special education students).

The goal in analyzing these variations is to uncover possible explanations for failure related to particular issues or practices that could potentially be explored more fully and identified for possible interventions. Different causes for student failure need different types of interventions. When rates of algebra course failure are more than 60 percent and attributable to incoming math skills, as we found in one district, students need supplementary instruction prior to algebra (but not the kind of retention in grade that has been shown to be associated with higher eventual dropout rates).[7] Students who are failing because of missing assignments need a different type of intervention. We will explore various change ideas that correspond to different causes of failure more fully in chapter 3.

Another type of analysis that would be extremely useful (but we have not yet seen in practice) involves delving into high school teacher gradebook data. Although we have been able to gain access to quarterly report card grades in some districts, these do not provide the level of detail that helps us to understand the process by which students arrived at those grades. We have been unable to gain access to analyze teacher gradebook data ourselves. And although much has been written about grading, we also have yet to identify any accounts of systematic analysis of teacher gradebook data except for a few isolated cases with very small samples.[8] We did hear briefly about a lower-tech version of this more than a decade ago, when one principal told us about her meeting with teachers to "open the gradebooks." She unfortunately did not go on to share many details, and soon left the principalship to take on other district leadership responsibilities. We did not see much evidence of her innovative analysis plan spreading to other schools. Perhaps she met substantial resistance. When we mentioned the idea of examining electronic teacher gradebook data more recently at a high school in a partner district, we encountered looks of incredulity from school leaders. They did not appear to believe they had any authority to request access to such data. It felt like we were asking them to invade teacher privacy.

If one can get past potential teacher resistance to this idea, one could use teacher gradebook data to explore the variation in the ways in which failing course grades are actually generated over time by the end of the semester or year (depending on how credits are earned within the particular district). One could explore the extent to which final failing grades were driven by missing assignments as opposed to particular assignment grades or tests and quizzes. One could examine the impact of different weighting systems and how those varied by subject area and teacher. One could determine points during the semester at which it becomes statistically impossible for students with particular posted grades to achieve a passing grade within the specified grade weighting system. (Rational actor students do stop trying at this point, once they realize it.) In short, one could begin to understand the variation in the processes that lead to failing grades, how those processes may be related to levels of course failure, and what kinds and levels of different interventions (for example, focusing on reducing missing assignments versus focusing on increasing assessment grades) are needed in different situations.

COLLECT AND ANALYZE INPUT DATA AND ITS RELATIONSHIP TO OUTCOMES

If analyses of ninth grade failure rates across schools identify schools that have lower than predicted rates of failure (based on incoming student characteristics), a useful part of the improvement process would involve some type of small-scale data collection (e.g., through interviews) to identify school practices that could potentially be related to these outcomes. For example, a school with lower than predicted failure rates could have implemented some type of monitoring and intervention system (missing in other schools) that could be helping to prevent a significant number of ninth grade course failures. Perhaps a school with lower than expected failure rates has higher rates of parental use of the district portal to monitor student assignment grades, and that might be linked to particular practices of the school to help increase parent portal usage rates.

One thing we discovered recently in a partner district was that some of the same demographic groups with disproportionately higher rates of ninth grade failure also have disproportionately lower rates of ninth grade families accessing the parent portal. These analyses used automatically collected data on login activity to parent portal accounts (as distinct from the student portal access accounts). We did conduct additional analyses controlling for prior failure and demographic factors associated with failure to ascertain whether the odds of student course failure were lower for those students whose families had accessed the parent portal.[9] Although we could not draw any causal conclusions, our findings of a significant negative relationship between parent portal usage and course failure, together with independent findings from an experimental study in another district conducted by other researchers, led us to encourage the district to consider interventions related to the parent portal as a possible change idea in the continuous improvement process (which we discuss in more detail in later chapters).

One could also explore other reasons for variation in failure rates within schools. Conversations with teachers with lower than expected failure rates could identify particular teacher practices in monitoring, feedback, or provision of relearning and reassessment opportunities that could explain differences. These might be worth deeper analytical exploration and wider discussion within the school.

The authors of *Learning to Improve* characterize this process of identifying practices that appear to be related to better outcomes as the work of "pursuing quality in standard work processes."[10] While this may be easier to envision when considering instructional processes, such as those in early literacy instruction, it is important to extend the work of continuous improvement to additional, noninstructional work processes such as systematic monitoring and timely interventions. It might even involve examining grading practices as "standard work processes" rather than leaving them completely up to autonomous teachers.

Analyzing the variation in student outcomes and the variation in the organizational inputs is a critical step as we seek to improve high school outcomes. But it needs to lead to a deeper analysis of the system within which all these factors are operating. It is to that important process of "seeing the system that produces the current outcomes" that we turn in the next chapter.[11]

CHAPTER 3

Considering the System That Produces High School Outcomes

Improvement science focuses attention on the critical role of the *systems* within which schools and the individuals within them (students and teachers and school leaders) are situated, and on how those systems contribute to producing the outcomes we observe. In this chapter we make specific recommendations for engaging in a process that will help you to "see the system that produces the current outcomes" and begin making a plan for testing improvement ideas around ninth grade course passing and credit accumulation.[1] This process will involve inviting multiple stakeholder groups to participate in root cause analysis, developing a "working theory of practice improvement," and identifying research-based change ideas for reducing student course failure.

Before we flesh out the steps one can follow to understand how the system contributes to producing ninth grade outcomes, let's consider a more general example of "seeing the system." Systems help to produce one phenomenon that has been noted in many schools throughout the United States: schools with high concentrations of students living in poverty also tend to have higher proportions of teachers who are less well qualified for teaching. This affects student outcomes in high school through the well-documented influence of teacher quality on those outcomes. Why does this inequitable distribution of teachers continue to occur even in districts where highly qualified candidates are applying for teaching positions?

Studies by the New Teacher Project identified systemic issues that could explain why so few of the highly qualified teachers who apply to teach in urban districts actually get hired by those districts.[2] They identified critical points in decision-making timelines that were slowing down the process so much that these qualified teachers decided to accept other positions outside those urban districts. Districts set deadlines for teacher departure decisions that were too late to be able to recruit highly qualified teachers to take their places. Union policies allowed teachers within the district to transfer to open positions, which further slowed down the hiring process for new teachers. District timelines pushed budgeting and forecasting too late in the timeline to be able to offer positions to highly qualified teachers in a timely way. Another study in a large urban district found inefficient practices within the district's human resources office that delayed the hiring process considerably. Candidates told of transcripts and other paperwork being lost not once, but multiple times. One principal specifically advised the kind of systems analysis emphasized in this continuous improvement principle, observing that "Processes and systems must be examined to get people through HR in a timely manner. HR must be [made] user friendly. They can start by just answering the phone—95 percent of the time I cannot get an answer."[3] Such findings should encourage education leaders to engage in a more systematic process of "seeing the system that produces the outcomes." The authors of *Learning to Improve* frame the process of seeing the system as "causal system analysis." Others have called this "root cause analysis."

INVITE MULTIPLE STAKEHOLDER GROUPS TO PARTICIPATE IN ROOT CAUSE ANALYSIS

Addressing the root causes of problems is an essential part of the continuous improvement process. The best way to do this is to engage in a systematic process of asking "Why?" Sometimes we can learn from the toddlers who drove us crazy by continuing to ask why. One continuous improvement approach, Six Sigma, promotes the "Five Whys" analysis that was developed by Sakichi Toyoda and used at Toyota Motors to get to the root causes of issues in the manufacturing process.[4] We can apply the same process to problems that schools encounter, such as high rates of ninth grade failure that have a negative effect on graduation rates.

We recommend engaging in this process of root cause analysis with multiple stakeholders, including district leaders, principals, teachers, parents, and students. This process is somewhat different from the listening sessions with multiple stakeholder groups we advocated in chapter 1. Those were designed to identify diverse perspectives on overarching goals for improvement and to facilitate the process of building consensus around those broad goals. Involving multiple stakeholder groups and their multiple perspectives in root cause analysis helps to ensure that you miss as few potential causes and solutions as possible. With the ideas we provide below as a resource for those convening such a group, we believe that useful ideas could be generated in a meeting of just two hours or so (though with more time available, the process could be even more valuable).

Leading Stakeholders Through the Five Whys Analysis

The first step in this process is to take members of stakeholder groups through the Five Whys process. This can lead to multiple explanatory scenarios for student failure. One can imagine the following Five Whys scenario:

> *Why do ninth grade students fail classes?*
> Because they received so many zeroes for missing assignments that their coursework average fell below 60.

This is the point at which many people stop asking questions. Haven't we explained why students are failing? Many of the discussions we have heard at this point devolve into: "They are lazy!! They don't want to do the work! They have earned the failing grade they received!"

But what if we continued and played out the full Five Whys process? We might have a more nuanced explanation that would suggest a possible improvement plan:

Why did they have so many missing assignments?
Because they were absent from class so many days during the semester and had missing assignments for each of those days.

Why were they absent from class so many days?
Because they were late to school and completely missed that first period class.

Why were they late to school?
Because they missed the bus.

Why did they miss the bus?
Because they didn't wake up in time to get ready and get to the bus stop.

Why didn't they wake up in time?
Is it because they are lazy (the conclusion most frequently jumped to)? Or because they are experiencing some kind of problem or trauma that interferes with their ability to get to bed and sleep at night?

One can also imagine alternate branches at certain points of the scenario that can lead to understanding other causes that merit addressing:

Why did they have so many missing assignments?
Because they are struggling with self-monitoring to complete work independently.

Why are they struggling with self-monitoring?

Because they have unaddressed mental health issues, or motivation issues, or family crisis issues, or other issues that need to be addressed.

Why are these issues unaddressed?
Because there is no systematic process in place to help diagnose reasons why students may have lots of missing assignments.

Why is there no systematic process in place?
Because school leaders have not yet identified the need for one.

Why have school leaders not yet identified this need?
Because they have not received guidance about the importance of having such systems in place.

The Five Whys analysis will also uncover other reasons for course failure. For example, another scenario might be:

Why do ninth grade students fail classes?
Because their extremely low grades on tests, quizzes, or other assignments (ranging from 0 to 40) caused their coursework average to fall below 60.

Why were their grades on tests and quizzes and assignments so low?
Because they usually did not complete all the questions on the quizzes and tests or all of the assignment.

Why did they not complete all the questions or all the work?
Because they were feeling so discouraged that they gave up.

Why did they give up?

At this point one can imagine alternative scenarios that would lead to different improvement strategies:

Because they had not studied sufficiently to be able to answer the questions.

> *or*
>
> Because they did not have the prior knowledge to be able to understand and do the coursework needed to master the course material or do the assignment.
>
> *or*
>
> Because they were struggling with personal issues that kept them from being able to focus on test questions or the assignment.
>
> *or*
>
> Because even when they had made a valiant effort in the past, they had received the message from teachers that they were a failure, and that effort wasn't worth it.

This is the point at which educators may begin to feel completely overwhelmed and somewhat defensive. They do not have the time and energy to learn about, much less deal with, all these problems that could be contributing to student failure. And how are these problems part of a system that produces the problem of course failure? Students didn't turn in assignments and/or they failed tests. This led to a grade below 60, and they failed the course.

A small wayside reflection at this point can help to illustrate how individual educational decisions can contribute to systemic problems. One of the most discouraging conversations we ever had with a teacher illustrates what many students face from grading systems that border on malpractice because of the way they lead to discouragement and shutdown. The conversation occurred during observations for an unrelated program evaluation study upon encountering a young middle school teacher in the break room. For some reason the teacher began recounting how she had given an assignment for students to submit a five-paragraph essay to help them prepare for the Common Core–aligned PARCC, the state's assessment test at the time. The teacher described how one student had submitted just a single paragraph. "Of course, I had to give him a zero, because he hadn't done the assignment," she related, with absolutely no understanding of what she had done. Given our researcher role at the school, we did not feel the freedom to say what needed to be said to her by an administrator: "How could you give a student who had actually tried and submitted at least some work on the assignment the same failing grade he would have received for doing nothing? Have you no idea what that does to student motivation? Have you considered why the student may only have been able to accomplish this much? What the student needs is some positive encouragement for what was accomplished and some constructive help in moving forward to accomplish the full assignment." But "seeing the system" in many districts reminds us that for the most part grading is left to teacher autonomy, and many teachers are not fully aware of the impact of grading practices on student motivation. Failures mount up when individual teachers can make decisions such as these without any systemic guidelines.

We encountered another grading situation that had a much happier ending because the school had a system in place for teachers to share information about students with each other. A math teacher in this school was telling her colleagues about a student who consistently missed the first period class. She would see him later each day at school, but he would never acknowledge her or tell her why he had missed math class. She found this disrespectful and told the group that she would be happy when she failed him. At this regularly scheduled meeting of teachers who shared the same cohort of students, the science teacher interjected: "Hold on! I know the reason why he is missing first period. He is taking his dad to chemotherapy in the mornings and is afraid if he tells anyone they will not let him do it." As soon as the math teacher was informed of the root cause of the student's absence, her attitude and approach rotated 180 degrees. She instead began thinking of ways to help the student overcome his challenges and pass the course. Without a system in place for teachers to regularly share insights about their common students, she would have happily failed the student, and the student would have felt further alienated from an "uncaring" school. In many cases this would have led to a downward spiral that would keep the student from graduating on time, if at all.

DEVELOP A WORKING THEORY OF PRACTICE IMPROVEMENT

Pausing regularly to ask the "why" questions is crucial for educators. Before we get into the nitty-gritty of helping stakeholders to see the system, it is important to summarize the findings from the Five Whys process in a way that will be useful in moving the process along. The Five Whys analysis is a first step in developing what improvement science researchers call a "fishbone diagram." Such a diagram summarizes some of the underlying causes or factors associated with the problem we are addressing.

In figure 3.1 we provide one possible summary of underlying factors associated with high school students failing courses; we developed this summary based on dialogues with stakeholders and participant observation of ninth grade improvement efforts in many schools over many years. Factors associated with school itself are clustered on the top of the diagram. Factors associated with the students themselves and their neighborhoods or families are along the bottom.

The figure portrays several school-related factors. Students may not have sufficient academic skills from prior grades' instruction to successfully master the course material. Students may not be exerting effort needed to pass courses for school-related reasons (they find school boring and irrelevant to life, or they may not feel like adults at the school really care about them). They may be missing school (and failing to turn in assignments) because they are fearful of bullying or worse from other students in the building. Grading systems may be very rigid with little opportunity to recover during the semester from early failing grades.

Along the bottom are some factors related to issues outside of school itself. Students may just not want to do the work of school—but this is often related to deeper issues. They may be experiencing neighborhood-related trauma or other personal problems that interfere with their ability to attend school or focus on learning and/or

FIGURE 3.1 Fishbone diagram for ninth grade failure

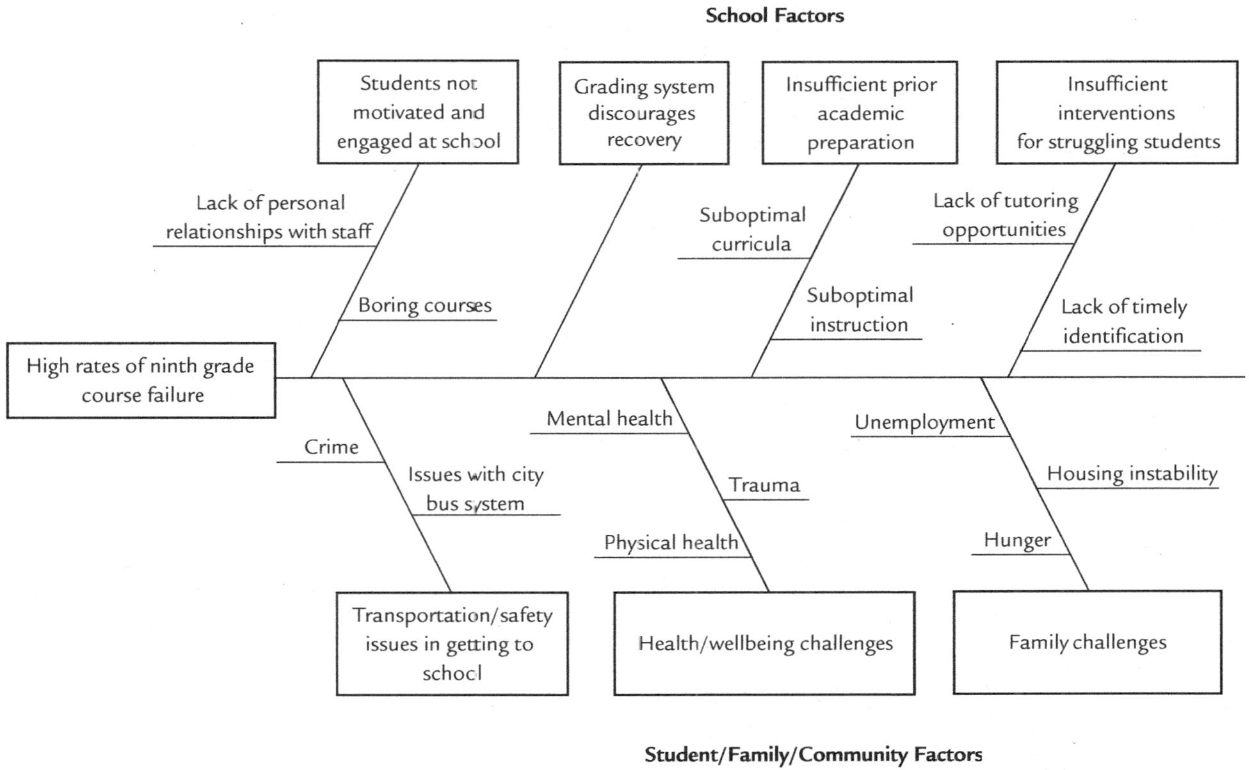

Note: This figure was inspired by the fishbone diagram in Bryk et al., *Learning to Improve*, 69.

completing assignments. They may be responding to learning difficulties and past school failures by simply shutting down. Or they may be missing school and therefore failing their classes for other reasons. There may be safety issues in getting to school, as one recent study in Baltimore has highlighted.[5] The city bus system that students rely on for getting to school may have big problems of its own that make it literally impossible for all students in the city to make it to school on time.[6] You can see how one could continue to expand the fishbone diagram.

Moving from Root Cause Analysis to Seeing the System

Stakeholders may have real difficulty in seeing the role of the system here in the same way that one could see it in the teacher hiring process example. How do we help people to see the system role? One way is to begin mapping out parts of the dynamic processes by which grades get determined, feedback occurs to students and families, and communication occurs (or does not occur) when warning signals about possible course failure begin to emerge. We present an example of this kind of mapping below.

Select Areas of Focus for the First Stages of Mapping

These areas of focus should emerge rather easily from the Five Whys analysis discussions. We identified several starting points: the classroom (teacher-student) system within which grades are created and some level of communication and intervention occurs, and the school-level and district-level systems which may have policies and practices related to grading, communication, and interventions. One might also consider external (noneducational) systems such as the city transportation system or the city social system that influence students' experiences in ways that relate to their school attendance.

Classroom level. One can imagine wide variation across teachers and classrooms in the ways in which teachers communicate expectations and details about grading systems to students, assign grades to these pieces of student work, communicate about those grades and provide feedback to students, provide interventions for students with low grades, calculate interim (report card) and final course grades, and communicate about these to students and families.

School level. Similarly, we have observed wide variation across schools in the extent to which policies are established and enforced, such as those for grading systems, providing timely feedback to students, providing interventions for students struggling with low grades, and providing timely communication with families about student grades (especially when they are trending low).

District level. District policies and practices can also affect ultimate outcomes in student course passing rates, with similar issues about grading systems, expectations of teachers for providing timely feedback to students, expectations of (and resources for) schools in providing interventions for students struggling with low grades, and communication with families about student grades (including the role of district-level systems such as parent portals).

Transportation. When school districts rely on transportation that is not under their own control (that is, outside the traditional "yellow bus" system), issues within that system can affect student outcomes. Relevant system components influencing student outcomes can include cost, lack of adequate alignment between available routes and student needs, transportation system challenges that affect on-time performance, and an inability to attend to safety issues for students using the transportation system.

Drafting a Systems Improvement Map

We graphically summarize the educational system components discussed above, related to the academic feedback system, in figure 3.2.[7] Constructing such a "systems improvement map" helps to identify places within a system where breakdowns could be occurring and where change ideas within work processes could potentially be introduced and tested for effectiveness in reducing failure rates. We predict that systems are not adequately ensuring that students who are showing patterns of failing grades early in a semester (predictive of later course failure) are receiving adequate interventions in a timely way to turn things around. Teachers may think they are intervening

FIGURE 3.2 System improvement map around academic feedback

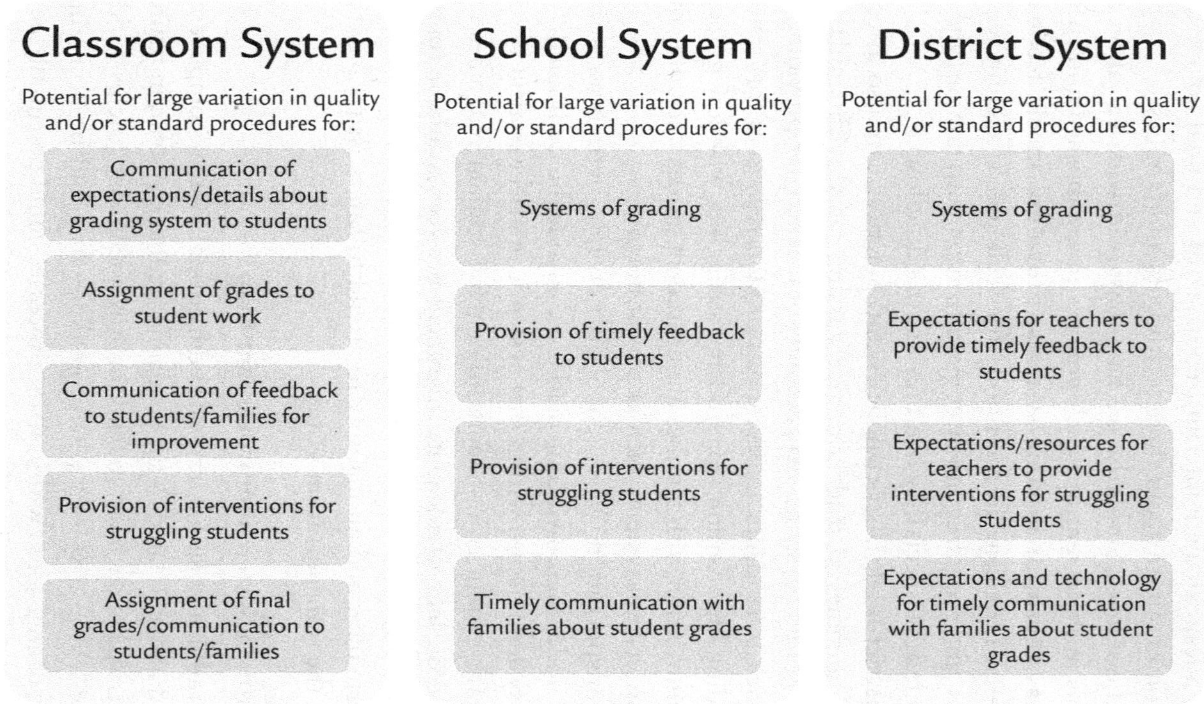

Note: This figure was inspired by the systems improvement map in Bryk et al., *Learning to Improve*, 71.

sufficiently (with reminders like "you owe me some assignments"), but if no one is probing about underlying problems that could help explain why the assignments continue to be "owed" but not delivered, there may be a system failure occurring.

This suggestion about system failure often evokes emphatic push-back from educators. "We are trying to teach responsibility. It is the student's responsibility to take initiative and talk about what is going on. It is not our responsibility to create systems to address this." Or educators balk at being expected to create systems that ensure the implementation of interventions to help students engage in the work needed to move from failure to success. Some may disagree that scarce resources should be allocated within a system to address a student failure issue. The trouble with this perspective is that the student's failure will become a systemic responsibility at some point. Most educational systems are now seeking to deal with the recovery of credits unearned due to course failure so that students can graduate from high school. If the educational system abdicates entirely in dealing with student failure, other social systems will deal with the consequences later. Failure must be approached as a systems problem.

Developing a Driver Diagram

Continuous improvement requires more than a summary of underlying causes and a system improvement map. We need to move toward making changes that could lead to improved outcomes. To support this practical focus, those working in improvement science have developed the "driver diagram." Driver diagrams summarize ideas about ways (or "drivers") to address underlying factors identified in the fishbone diagram—drivers that might actually help to achieve a specific and measurable improvement goal. It forces us to get specific about what we are trying to achieve and how we are going to get there. In figure 3.3 we provide an example related to our problem of ninth grade course failure.

We have a problem of course failure that we want to reduce. It's important to set a specific goal. The specific size of the goal for reducing course failure among ninth graders (by how many percentage

FIGURE 3.3 Simplified driver diagram for reducing ninth grade course failure

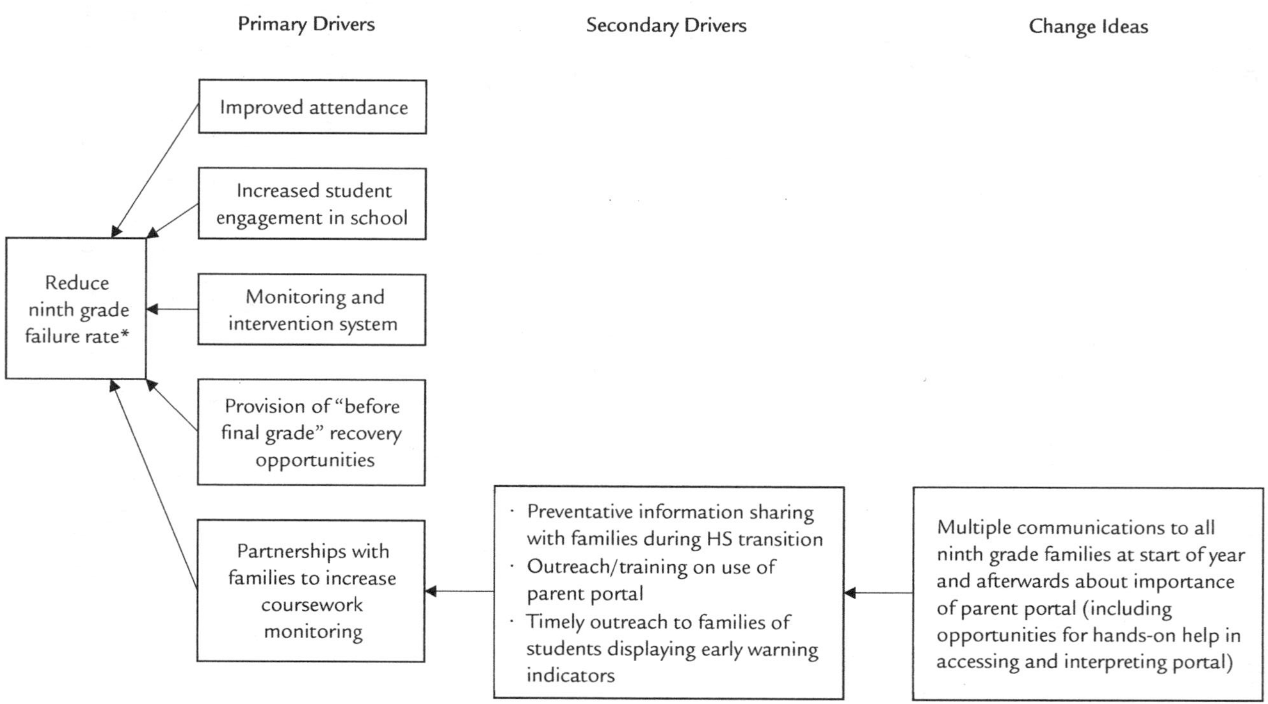

**Note:* This figure was inspired by the driver diagram in Bryk et al., *Learning to Improve*, 78. A more complex driver diagram would specify secondary drivers and change ideas for all primary drivers. The Aim Statement would ideally have a specific goal for the percentage reduction and the date by which this would be accomplished.

points over what period of time) needs to vary depending on the size of the problem in each particular context. It is crucial to aim at a sweet spot between a goal that is attainable in real world conditions and ambitious enough to provoke significant changes in standard work processes at a scale large enough to make a meaningful difference. It may take considerable discussion among stakeholders to determine what this goal should be and what kind of progress the group needs to aim at to help build the momentum to sustain the work.

After these discussions we can settle on a set of drivers, associated with particular change ideas, which could potentially help us reach that goal. Figure 3.3 portrays a multifaceted driver diagram that summarizes factors associated with many different kinds of interventions that could potentially go on in an entire system (probably at a much later stage than in a setting where a continuous improvement effort is just getting started). A particular continuous improvement team would probably be working on just one particular driver or even one specific component of a driver at a time. So as figure 3.3 indicates, in an ideal case there would be teams working on all these (and other) factors: improving student attendance rates, increasing student engagement in school, monitoring low grades and implementing interventions, providing recovery opportunities, and building partnerships with families to increase monitoring of student course performance.

In figure 3.4 we provide another example of a driver diagram for course performance from our Gates Foundation–funded Networks for School Improvement (NSI) work with City Year. In this collaborative work with school teams, we identified five overarching drivers: data, relationships, mindsets, skills, and practices. The data driver involves several components: access to and monitoring of data by teachers, students, and families; systematic analysis of data by school teams; and using data to drive instruction. Within the relationships driver we identified several secondary drivers, including specific ways of leveraging student-teacher and student-student relationships to increase student effort. The mindsets driver includes secondary drivers related to active learning, growth mindset, and self-advocacy. Several secondary drivers are also indicated within the skills driver, and under the practices driver we outline several specific actions or activities within classrooms or schools that have been shown to be promising in our previous work.

IDENTIFY RESEARCH-BASED CHANGE IDEAS

The process of identifying secondary drivers helps lead to more specific interventions and change ideas that may lead to improvements in particular factors linked to course performance. In identifying specific change ideas, it is important to build on what others have learned in the past about effective (and not so effective) practices or interventions. Table 3.1 provides an inventory of change ideas related to the drivers for course performance, developed in our NSI work with schools in Milwaukee.

As we proceed to the nitty-gritty stages of the continuous improvement process in the final three improvement principles, we want to propose five broad change idea umbrellas—with considerable research evidence—that are relevant for addressing the problem of ninth grade course performance. These five umbrellas are:

- implementing and monitoring early warning and intervention systems;
- engaging families to support ninth grade students;
- increasing students' sense of connectedness to school;
- improving important noncognitive skills through social-emotional learning interventions;
- transforming teacher instructional practices to motivate and engage students more deeply in academic work.

We will use examples from these change ideas as we provide practical guidance in the areas of measurement for improvement, disciplined inquiry, and accelerating learning through networked communities. Before moving into these components of the continuous improvement process in the following chapters, however, it will be useful to review some of the evidence about these broad change ideas. Because continuous improvement often focuses on improving

FIGURE 3.4 Primary and secondary drivers for course performance (from Networks for School Improvement project with City Year in Milwaukee)

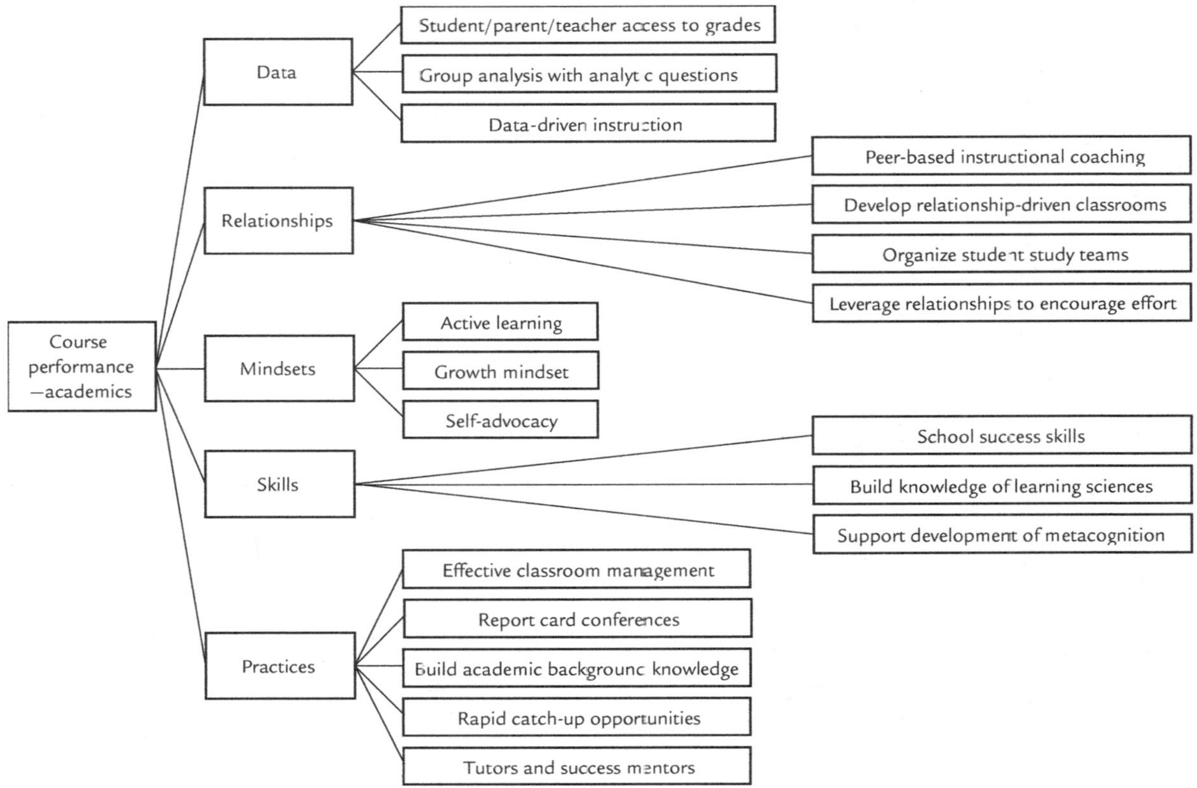

work processes, we will also delve a bit more deeply in the remainder of this chapter into the systems and work processes associated with the change ideas listed above.

Implementing and Monitoring Early Warning and Intervention Systems

There is a frequently told fable about villagers who spent a great deal of time rescuing individuals they noticed flailing in the river that flowed through the center of their town.[8] Eventually they determine that the upstream bridge is full of holes. The fable reminds us that instead of focusing all our attention on trying to intervene with failing students, we need to go upstream to address why students are falling through the cracks in the first place.

TABLE 3.1 Course performance improvement inventory

Data

☐ Do student/parent/teacher teams have access to grades in progress—it is important that all of these groups have as close to real time understanding of current student success across all courses.

☐ Have teacher teams conducted group analysis with analytic questions? In order to understand why groups of students are not doing well in a course, teachers and adults who know the student should ask and answer four questions. Do students:

a) focus in class
b) comprehend material
c) complete assignments
d) show what they know on assessments

Then do teacher teams use the answers to formulate and test hypotheses?

☐ Have you implemented data-driven instruction—including use of formative assessments, exit tickets, etc., and time built into the school week to analyze, reflect, and act on the data?

Relationships

☐ Have you used a relationship-driven approach to teacher improvement centered on peer-based instructional coaching and Professional Learning Communities to reduce teacher isolation, encourage the use of more effect instructional techniques, and build collective efficacy?

- ☐ Have you supported teachers in the development of relationship-driven classrooms with challenging and caring learning environments, by helping them identify and build the know-how to do so?
- ☐ Have you organized supportive student study teams?
- ☐ Have you leveraged supportive relationships with students to encourage C students and below to put forth full effort?

Mindsets

- ☐ Have you built both teacher and student belief and competence in using active learning techniques,such as Socratic seminars, cooperative learning, project- and problem-based learning, etc.?
- ☐ Have you built both student and teacher belief that effort leads to success and that everyone can learn?
- ☐ Have you provided opportunities for students to develop success scripts—experiences where they learn from mistakes and understand the amount of effort needed to succeed?
- ☐ Have you built both student and teacher belief that it is important, acceptable, and encouraged to advocate for the supports and environments needed for a student to learn?

Skills

- ☐ Have you taught students the underlying skills needed to succeed in school, such as study skills, time management, active listening, collaboration, etc.?
- ☐ Have you built up teacher knowledge of the Learning Sciences and how to teach for long-term recall and knowledge integration (e.g., engineering active recall, elaboration, gist, etc.)?
- ☐ Have you supported the development of metacognition—the ability to be reflective on how learning occurs or learn how to learn?

Practices

- ☐ Effective classroom management
- ☐ Have you on a quarterly basis had students receive one-on-one conferences on their report cards from caring adults who are not their primary teachers?
- ☐ Have you built academic background knowledge?
- ☐ Have you implemented a rapid catch-up or assignment completion opportunities support by adults—providing students with fair and reasonable means to make up missed assignments with adult support?
- ☐ Have you provided students who are struggling in a class with a success coach or a tutor, depending on if the primary challenge is social-emotional or academic?

Total ____

Early warning and intervention (EWI) systems have become a widely implemented approach to improving student graduation outcomes in response to research findings from the mid-2000s.[9] Using longitudinal student cohort data, those studies identified several behavioral factors as the strongest predictors of high school graduation. In contrast to demographic characteristics that schools could not address, the factors of student attendance, behavior, and course performance were behaviors that could potentially be changed by timely interventions. Educational organizations (including Achieve, America's Promise Alliance, the Alliance for Education, the National High School Center, the Mid-Atlantic Equity Consortium, and SEDL) translated those findings into practical advice for district and school leaders through early warning system handbooks and briefs.[10] By 2016, over half of public high schools in a nationally representative survey reported that they had implemented an early warning system.[11] Findings from several large randomized studies have found better student outcomes in attendance and course performance at schools that were implementing a systematic early warning and intervention process than schools continuing with business as usual.[12] But there is considerable variation across schools in how well such systems are implemented and whether they produce improved student results. As the 2016 survey indicated, less than half the high schools claiming to have an early warning system had "frequently coordinated" that system with services and strategies within the school to help struggling students.[13] It is important to consider how to improve the working of such systems so that they will reliably yield improved student outcomes. To do that, one can implement an EWI system improvement mapping process.

Flowchart the Current Attendance Monitoring System

Although we may be primarily interested in ensuring the effectiveness of a monitoring system for *course grades*, we need to begin by emphasizing the need for a monitoring and intervention system around one of the primary determinants of course grades—student attendance. While the correlation isn't perfect, and varies from school to school, one of the best predictors of course grades is student attendance rate. Low rates of attendance are highly correlated with low course grades. If the school is not monitoring and intervening around attendance issues in a timely way, it will have difficulty seeing success in reducing course failure rates. The most recent federal data on chronic absenteeism (from 2018) shows that many more high school students are missing significant amounts of schooling than is commonly assumed. In nearly a third of all high schools (including regular, vocational, and alternative high schools) 30 percent or more of high school students missed essentially a month or more of school.[14]

One of the first questions school leaders need to consider is how well they are monitoring and intervening to prevent chronic absence. This involves intervention during the first month of school. Students who miss more two or more days of school during the first month are missing 10 percent or more of school days and are by most definitions at risk of being chronically absent during the year. Research has shown that "September matters" and that schools need to have effective intervention strategies in place from the very first month of school to ensure that students are attending enough to be able to pass their courses.[15] This would involve personal contact with both the student and the family during that critical first month of school and throughout the year to address this issue. Shared information from the middle school about students already manifesting chronic absence problems could guide important outreach from the high school to build relationships with those students and families prior to the beginning of the ninth grade year. Depending on the size of the attendance problem at a school, this first step may be the primary change idea that the school needs to implement and evaluate before addressing any more course failure related issues.

The needs assessment around attendance systems may be more complex than you think, as schools may mistakenly think they have this base covered. Many schools already have a system in place that automatically contacts the parent any time a student is absent from school. Platforms like School Messenger allow parents to set preferences about how they want to be contacted. But such systems depend on the accuracy of the phone number or email address in the system, and sometimes on whether or not the parent has opted into the platform. One of the first issues a school leadership team should consider is how well any existing system is working to ensure that all families are actually receiving communications. Do the existing systems provide data on nonworking numbers? Is there a feedback loop that helps schools to replace nonworking numbers with accurate ones? Does the system allow for parental response to indicate whether the message was received? Schools may be relying on systems that are not actually successfully communicating with families about absences.

Because personal contact is an important dimension of the positive relationships with school staff that have been shown to be significantly related to student outcomes, it is important to consider how ensuring personal outreach to all students missing two or more days in a thirty day calendar period is being (or can be) implemented. This involves questions of how data will be generated and shared with individuals who have been given the responsibility to make that personal contact with students. How will the status of this contact be recorded in a datafile? How will school leaders ensure the positive quality of the interaction through their selection and training of appropriate staff members for this responsibility? How will information that can inform intervention strategies, as well as the interventions themselves, be recorded, monitored, and analyzed? If any of these links in the system is missing or weak, there is an opportunity to make changes that could improve the system's effectiveness.

School leaders must also make decisions about a system to ensure personal (rather than automated) contact with families after a certain number of absences. Are all the steps in place to document whether the communication occurred, what information was gained, what other interventions were selected, when they were implemented, and what the result was? How are those data analyzed so they can inform decision-making? Because attendance has such a large effect on student course performance, schools cannot afford to ignore these questions.

Flowchart the Current Course Performance Monitoring System

School leaders may also believe that they are doing a good job in monitoring course performance. All schools have some level of course performance monitoring if students receive quarterly report cards. The grades students receive on that first quarter report card are sometimes the first signal to them and to their families that things are going ok—or that they are not ok. Some schools even have a progress monitoring report several weeks prior to the end of first quarter. It may only tell them whether they are passing or failing (as is the case in one district we know), but it does count as some sort of systemic alert mechanism about course performance. A first step for school teams as they consider whether changes in their monitoring systems could be beneficial to students is to map or flowchart out the particular things that happen over the timeline of the semester to help students and their families keep track of their performance. This will help to identify holes or missing links in the system. It is also critical to superimpose on this flowchart the relevant information about how intervention strategies are—or are not—being systematically implemented.

As you begin mapping the major systematic steps in place, you need to probe more deeply into the details of communication systems. For example, say that during first semester the following things are in place:

- Quarter 1 progress report 5 weeks
- Quarter 1 report card 9 weeks
- Quarter 2 progress report 14 weeks
- Semester 1 report card 18 weeks

The next step is to outline communication steps around these reports with students and families.

Do families receive communication (for example, a robocall) to let them know that reports have been distributed? (And do you know if the robocall was answered, even if you cannot tell whether it was the parent or child who answered?) Are grade reports posted in an online portal in an easily readable format or sent directly to families, or do families have to request them from the students? Are there systems in place that ensure that all students (or at least those with grades below a certain level) have conversations with supportive adults at the school who can help them probe into reasons for low grades and plan strategies that will help them improve? Are there systems in place that ensure that families are informed personally and actually communicate directly with school personnel about ways they can support their student's success? Does this all depend on individual teacher discretion, or are there school-level systems that ensure that these communications happen for all students who need them?[16]

Once you have mapped out these details about the existence of communication systems, it is essential to analyze how the school manages data about how these communication systems are working. Who manages datafiles with information about students who are struggling at the week five progress report stage? Is there a system in place to enter data on the personal conversation that occurs between that student and a school staff member, and what follow-up occurs after that conversation? Likewise, is there a data system in place to track communications with the family? If these data systems are not in place at the school, this would probably be the place to begin introducing a change and using disciplined inquiry to analyze whether that change leads to improvement in ninth grade course passing. If the very idea of creating these data systems provokes objections from school staff, it may be necessary to build understanding about the need for data about interventions to evaluate whether the interventions are working and make decisions about revising intervention plans.

Study the Functioning of the Existing Monitoring and Intervention System

Perhaps all these data systems are indeed in place at your school. The next question focuses on how the data are being analyzed and discussed, and what you are learning from those analyses. How many conversations with struggling students—and follow-up interactions—actually happen (and how does this vary by different factors, including student and staff characteristics)? What interventions actually take place and what is the result? Analyses of these data can lead to conclusions about what changes can be tried in the next stage of the continuous improvement process. Once you have analyzed the systems and work processes in your own school setting, you will be ready to embark on more specific cycles of inquiry to investigate whether and how a particular change or set of changes you select actually makes a difference in your school. After discussing relevant measurement issues in chapter 4, we will provide specific practical guidance in chapter 5 for how you and your team can engage in systematic, disciplined inquiry to drive improvement.

Engaging Families as Partners in Supporting Ninth Grade Success

Research has firmly established a link between levels of family involvement and support and children's educational outcomes at the secondary as well as the primary level.[17] Factors such as high expectations for children's educational attainment, communication about schoolwork and other topics, monitoring of homework, and a supportive and structured parenting style are strongly associated with higher levels of student achievement. Other research studies have shown that this is not just a static relationship between family characteristics and student outcomes. Efforts by schools to systematically organize their family engagement efforts and increase their communications and interactions with families can make a difference in increasing effective family support to students and improving student outcomes. School efforts to increase and improve the ways they engage with families have been linked to improved attendance outcomes.[18] Communication strategies that keep families apprised of student progress and proactively address misbeliefs they may hold have been shown in randomized studies to have a positive effect on student outcomes.[19] Research has shown that the more frequently schools contact families about homework, the more frequently families talk with their children about it.[20]

But just as students are making the critical transition to high school and entering the "make or break" year of ninth grade, high schools tend to place less priority on engaging families than lower-level schools, and family engagement declines precipitously as a result.[21] Monitoring support from teachers also tends to decline during that critical year, according to research findings.[22] Schools and districts may be working on interventions like early warning systems at the school level, but considerably fewer are also seeking to improve high school engagement of families as allies to provide the monitoring many ninth grade students need to successfully pass their courses.

Audit Family Engagement Work Processes

In order to identify some of the "holes in the bridge" that can explain why students may be falling through the cracks and failing by the end of the first quarter, it is also important for schools to assess their family engagement efforts to understand where there may be gaps in communications processes. If families are not receiving all the information they may need to be able to effectively support their adolescents during the transition to high school, student outcomes could be suffering as a result. As one ninth grade parent we encountered put it, "We don't know what we don't know." School leaders need to ensure that the important information that is related to student success is communicated effectively to families as well as to students.

It is crucial for a school team to flowchart the timeline and processes in place for communicating with families to identify how gaps in the information flow may be occurring. What modes of communication are used, and who may not be receiving the intended communications? To what extent are there multiple opportunities to obtain important information? Is the school actively disseminating information that families need to help their teens to be successful? (Do all families understand the importance of course grades for earning course credits, and the relationship between attendance and course passing? Do they understand the rules about making up work during absences? Do they know how to contact teachers, how to get tutoring help, etc.?) Ideally, high schools will have a "family engagement team" that includes student and parent representatives, as Joyce Epstein and the National Network of Partnership Schools recommend.[23] Students and family members can help school leaders to see their communication system through the eyes of those it is designed to reach, and help to point out the holes in the bridge.

Increasing Student Connectedness to School

Building early warning systems and engaging families more effectively to ensure students attend regularly and receive the help they need when struggling academically are critical for increasing student success in high school. But students need a reason for going to school. They need a sense of belonging—to know that they are cared for by adults at school and have positive relationships with peers. Students need to believe they are welcomed, wanted, cared about, and needed in their school. They need to feel that school policies are fair, supportive, and just. They need to know that they are known, and to be able to find peers with similar interests, outlooks, and experiences. They want to have the sense that they are able to help others. These factors are key for predicting what has been termed school connectedness—the belief that school is a place you want to be.[24]

What factors can increase this sense of school connectedness? Positive relationships are critical—but they cannot be taken for granted. Our experience over decades of observations in schools has shown us that adults in schools have considerable room for growth in this area. Students may not be angels, but it is often the adults who commit "assumicide" and precipitate unnecessarily negative interactions. There are steps that adults can take to create more positive communication and an atmosphere that makes school more of a place where everyone wants to be. A simple intervention involving teachers greeting students at the door of the classroom has been shown to have a positive effect on student engagement and positive classroom behavior.[25]

Other research has identified the importance of extracurricular activities in helping students feel connected to school.[26] Such activities can create venues for students to engage in positive peer relationships, develop a sense of competency and success in particular areas, and enjoy the satisfaction of helping others and making a difference in their community. At times these activities may tip the scales in a student's decision to attend school or not on a particular day. And they even contribute to students' postsecondary education applications. They make a difference.

Taking stock of how well the school is doing in building this sense of connectedness is an important step in "seeing the system that is producing the problem." This could begin with simple counts of positive and negative interactions between adults and students overheard in the offices and hallways. It could progress to include analysis of the extracurricular activities available to students and identification of students that may not be connected to any of those activities. In chapter 5 we will explore in greater detail how schools could identify and assess the impact of particular ideas to make improvement in school connectedness.

Improving Noncognitive Skills Through Social-Emotional Learning

Research has shown that the student success in courses needed for high school graduation and college enrollment is linked not only to attendance but also to noncognitive skills associated with self-management like self-regulation, goal-directed behavior, and personal responsibility.[27] Similarly, workplace success relies on these skills as well as social awareness and relationship skills.[28] This suggests the need for better approaches to help prepare students for the challenges of the high school environment where students typically have more independence and personal responsibility and receive less teacher support.[29] Moreover, recent research has shown that two important dimensions of social and emotional learning—self-management and self-efficacy—tend to decline during middle school and so it is particularly important to bolster these orientations by the first year in high school.[30]

There is growing evidence that providing interventions that build students' social-emotional learning and other noncognitive skills results in positive growth not only in behavior and attitudes, but also in academic performance.[31] The recent Aspen Commission on Social, Emotional, and Academic Development has made the case for an integrated approach to student development in which social-emotional and cognitive development are intertwined to propel student success in school and out.[32] In particular, learning activities that emphasize developing a growth mindset, social belonging, and purpose in learning have shown evidence of improving high school outcomes.[33]

Monitoring the status of student social-emotional development, as several districts in California are working together to do, is an important first step for making progress.[34] Student self-report measures are probably the easiest way to collect data and can yield helpful and reliable findings. In chapter 5 we will explore how schools might implement and study the impact of particular change ideas related to improving particular noncognitive skills and mindsets.

Improving Instructional Practices to Motivate and Engage Students

There is a relatively high degree of consensus among education researchers about the relationship between certain instructional practices and student academic outcomes. Although some instructional practices and measures of instructional quality are specific to particular content areas or skills, there are general practices that span most content areas at the high school level.[35] Positive teacher-student relationships, characterized by warmth and support, are positively related to higher student engagement and achievement, particularly for secondary school students and students coming from lower socioeconomic status backgrounds.[36] Positive relationships among students in the classroom have also been shown to be associated with better student outcomes. Classroom environments need to address students' deep need for belonging to a supportive community. At the same time, social support needs to be balanced with academic rigor and challenging instruction.[37] Students tend to perform better when they are provided more choices and autonomy.[38] Helping students to see the relevance of classroom learning for their current lives and future work leads to better performance.[39] Students are much more engaged in learning and motivated to put forth their best effort when they are working on meaningful projects addressing critical problems facing their local and global communities.[40] Such project-based learning can help them develop the critical thinking and communication skills that will prepare them for work and citizenship. Practices that allow students to track and experience their own growth in mastery or competence have been associated with more positive student outcomes.[41] Students who are given the opportunity and encouragement to relearn and improve their work assignments tend to rise to the opportunity and demonstrate mastery while those assessed under systems without these opportunities often become discouraged and give up.

Our long experience with high schools and districts has taught us that historically underserved ninth grade students rarely have the opportunity to experience engaging hands-on project-based learning and career-oriented coursework. These courses are generally not available to students until later in their high school years (after they have experienced academic course failure, fallen off track to graduation, and often have to sacrifice career-oriented coursework to make up academic credits that were not earned earlier). Having shadowed students throughout the school day, we understand why many ninth graders need a compelling reason to come to school. They need to understand how what they are learning actually matters in the real world. They need a chance to experience the joy of learning and simply have fun as they learn. One of the change ideas we explore briefly in chapter 5 involves implementing project-based learning (and in particular, a robotics course) for ninth graders to build enthusiasm about learning in the rest of their core courses.

Identify Where Change May Be Needed in Instructional Practices

A combination of classroom observations and more comprehensive student surveys can help to identify specific areas where classroom instructional practices may need improvement. Gathering and analyzing teacher descriptions of their grading systems is also a helpful step in mapping the landscape and identifying areas where change ideas could be implemented and studied. Such a whole-school, systemic approach to conducting a needs assessment can complement individual department efforts to improve specific content-related instructional practices.

Analyzing the "inputs" to teachers around instructional practice is another component of understanding the work processes within the system. What professional development opportunities have been available to teachers, and in what training activities have they actually engaged? How much preparation time do they have, and how are they using it? How much teacher collaboration is occurring, and who is involved? Understanding the system surrounding teachers' instructional practice is critical for any improvement efforts that may be undertaken.

Moving Forward in Continuous Improvement

We will explore in chapter 5 the nitty-gritty task of using "disciplined inquiry to drive improvement" through each of these large change idea umbrellas. Our plan is to provide models of specific improvement processes that can be a practical guide to follow and adapt in your own educational context. But before we get to that step, we need to discuss a crucial factor in the improvement process—the issue of *measuring* whether or not improvement is really taking place. It is to that critical issue of measurement that we now turn in chapter 4.

CHAPTER 4

How Can We Measure Change So We Know If Improvement Is Occurring?

How will you know if a change leads to improvement? Bryk and his colleagues rightly remind us that we "cannot improve at scale what we cannot measure."[1] They also emphasize that the outcome measures that we focus so much attention upon are not always useful as measures in the improvement process. To be sure, it is crucial to determine if there is ultimate improvement in the outcomes we are seeking to improve. Did attendance rates increase, and chronic absence go down? Are students learning more? Have we been successful at increasing the percentage of students who have earned all their ninth grade credits and are on track to on-time graduation?

But waiting for yearly measures is not generally useful in the improvement process itself. And it becomes very difficult to determine if particular change efforts made a difference in the final yearly outcome when there may be many interventions going on simultaneously. We need additional measures that can help us to assess improvement.

Before we go on to consider the disciplined inquiry needed in the continuous improvement process (chapter 5), it is crucial to explore this issue of measurement that is so central in the process. As we consider measures that could potentially be helpful in gauging the impact of our improvement efforts, we find it useful to distinguish among several different types of measures. In the rest of this chapter we will consider types of interim outcome data, measures of "process functioning," and perception measures. School and district leaders might prefer to call these measures of short-term student outcomes, the intervention process, and student attitudes and beliefs. Our goal is to help you identify practical improvement measures for potential change ideas that are useful in the improvement process and possible to measure with resources available within schools.

INTERIM OUTCOME DATA (SHORT-TERM STUDENT OUTCOMES)

The most important student outcome measures we are trying to improve are often yearly measures: what were a student's final course grades, and did they earn the needed credits for graduation? This is what appears on the transcript that colleges see. But these outcome data are greatly influenced by interim measures, like quarterly report card grades. And those are influenced by assignment grades, and often by whether or not assignments were submitted.

If we want to examine whether changes or interventions are leading to improvement in shorter cycles than an entire year, it is important to use these interim measures. Those involved in the continuous improvement effort need to collaboratively identify meaningful interim measures that are practical to collect and analyze.

One might begin with what is relatively easy for teachers to track in their online gradebooks. If failure to submit classwork or homework assignments has been identified as a contributing factor to student failure, one might want to track the extent to which there was an increase in the percentage of students submitting classwork or homework assignments after implementation of a particular change, such as offering more choice or more creative assignments, or offering opportunities for students to get the help they need to even try a homework assignment. If the change idea involved increased tutoring opportunities and outreach to struggling students, did this result in a decrease of failing quarter grades (compared to a similar group not receiving the intervention)?

Similarly, if improvement efforts are focused on increasing attendance, one could track short-term changes in (already collected) attendance rates over time after a particular intervention. Comparing the intervention group to a similar group, one can test whether greeting students daily at the classroom door to let them know they are valued and cared for works in your particular context, as it has elsewhere. And one can determine whether it works as well or better than more extrinsic incentives (such as rewards like pizza parties for the homeroom with best attendance).

Measuring improvement in particular academic skills (beyond reading and mathematics, for which there are numerous assessments) or social-emotional learning is somewhat more complicated as an interim outcome measure. Here it is important to build on the hard work of others rather than seeking to reinvent measures that may already exist in a usable or adaptable format. The National Writing Project used a continuous improvement approach in developing a tool to measure students' skill in argumentative writing, the "Using Sources Tool."[2] The American Council on the Teaching of Foreign Languages has developed a comprehensive set of performance indicators for world languages.[3] Other groups, notably charter school networks, have been developing assessments of twenty-first-century skills.[4] For example, Learn with Two Rivers posts its rubrics for measuring effective reasoning, decision-making, and problem-solving.[5] Summit Public Schools has a "Habits of Success" measure that includes components of emotional intelligence, self-directed learning, learning strategies, academic mindsets, and school and classroom culture.[6] We have also had success using the Devereux Student

Strengths Assessment–Mini (DESSA-mini) behavior rating scale, a measure of students' social-emotional competence that is completed by classroom teachers.[7]

Of course, it is crucial to examine the more consequential summary outcomes (final course grades) as well, since short-term outcomes need to be sustained to make a difference. But measuring interim outcomes can provide an early indication that what we thought might be an effective intervention does not seem to be having the kind of impact needed to make a difference in the long run.

PROCESS (INTERVENTION) MEASURES

Bryk and colleagues remind us that much of what we need to consider in improving our schools and educational systems relates to standard work processes.[8] Research findings about effective instruction in various content areas have led to specific steps or microprocesses that should be occurring on a regular basis. Similarly, research on early warning systems has begun to identify particular steps or processes that are important for those systems to function effectively and yield the intended results. Flowcharting processes to understand where problems are occurring can help to identify specific steps in standard work processes that need particular attention.[9] Focusing attention on those steps in the process helps to illuminate particular process measures that need to be collected and analyzed.

Consider, for example, standard work processes around absenteeism. One step that is often overlooked is the process by which teachers record student attendance in the classroom (and when those data become available for monitoring and guiding interventions). One important process measure is the percentage of teachers who record attendance for each class period. This could be affected by technical or other difficulties (internet access issues, classroom management or organizational routine issues, etc.). Another standard work process involves communication with families about attendance. In our experience schools may have a system for early intervention, such as robocalls to families to let them know about student absence sometime during the morning. But whether that even has a chance to be effective depends heavily on the extent to which the school actually has up-to-date contact information for families. What percentage of those calls are not actually reaching the right phone number? What percentage of families have opted in to receive text messages (an often more effective means of communication than phone calls that cannot be answered during a parent's workday)? These kinds of process measures may often be overlooked.

One can identify additional process measures related to monitoring and intervention processes around absenteeism and failing grades. If an intervention goal of a personal conversation with a school adult every time a student misses two days or more within a month is identified, a process needs to be in place to ensure records are kept of absences and interventions. This can generate a measure of the percentage of absent students who received check-ins with an adult. Similarly, another process measure would be the percentage of students with failing first quarter grades who had a meeting with a school adult.

Another process that schools might seek to encourage with families is having parents check the online parent portal on a regular basis to keep informed about their child's progress. On the school side, this would involve communicating with families about how to do this. One possible process measure could involve the number of communications that were made. A more precise measure would include information about the extent to which messages were received (that is, it would indicate nonworking email addresses or phone numbers). To measure the extent to which school communications about the portal led to families accessing the portal, the school would need district support in reporting back data on family logins to the portal. This could become a standard work process at the district level.

In order for the portal to be useful to students and families, it needs to be updated by teachers on a regular basis. Another type of standard work process measurement that is important to consider is the percentage of classroom sections for which up-to-date information on grades is available on a regular basis (updated at least every two weeks, for example). This could be contentious to implement, and could require specific programming to generate the needed data. But it is critical to be able to measure and assess how the process of keeping students and families informed about student progress is being implemented. It is not possible for students or families to respond to feedback or warning signals in a timely way if they are not available in a timely way.

These are just a few examples of process measures. As the improvement team considers the system and how it is influencing outcomes, they will inevitably notice other work processes that need to be measured—and implemented, if they are not routinely conducted already.

PERCEPTION (STUDENT ATTITUDE) MEASURES

As we probe more deeply into the root causes of student struggles in attendance and course performance, and as we seek to make changes that address these, we need to find ways to measure whether those changes are improving student experiences in school. But finding *doable* ways to collect reliable data to measure improvement in such areas as teacher instructional practices is a challenge. Teachers can videotape their practice, but where do we find the time (except in funded studies) for trained observers to code and analyze the video data and draw conclusions? Administrators barely have time for one observation per teacher per year. Instead of relying on "objective" measures that are difficult to collect, we can begin by measuring changes in student perceptions.

Research on student perceptions of classroom teaching has shown that student survey measures are valid and useful for capturing students' instructional experiences.[10] The Project for Education Research That Scales (PERTS) has developed a student survey measurement tool that could be useful in short-cycle improvement efforts.[11] It consists of short student survey batteries that measure student perceptions of key characteristics of effective learning communities: teacher caring, classroom belonging, student voice, meaningful work, feedback for growth, and affirming cultural identity. These short surveys take just five to ten minutes and can be conducted and analyzed easily, especially if responses are collected digitally to avoid the additional step of creating usable datafiles. (This does require computer technology that may not be available in many schools, though teachers can leverage students' smart phones if those are more widely available.) Teachers are able to measure student perceptions of these classroom characteristics over time to test whether their use of change ideas or new (research-recommended) practices actually make a difference in how students are experiencing the classroom. Research by PERTS has also linked changes in student perceptions of the classroom environment to improved student academic performance, though it is important for these findings to be replicated in other contexts. Wording of the survey questions is posted on the PERTS website. PERTS also offers a Copilot-Elevate professional learning program that provides teachers with reports of student survey results, as well as lists of research-based change practices that teachers can try out and a system for tracking their improvement over time.[12] Case studies on their website highlight some of the positive results teachers have experienced in using these tools.

Another group of student survey measures is available from the California CORE districts that have been engaging in continuous improvement work.[13] These include several social-emotional learning measures (for self-efficacy, growth mindset, self-management, and social awareness) as well as various school climate measures (supports for academic learning, school connectedness, and safety). CORE also provides information on validity and reliability for these measures, though they may not have been used in short-cycle improvement efforts to the same extent as the PERTS measures.

In the appendix we propose a list of additional student survey items that could be piloted in the spirit of the PERTS Copilot-Elevate program to measure other student perceptions. We include student perception measures of their school connectedness, behavioral engagement, interest in schoolwork, and the relevance of schoolwork. The items in the appendix also include measures of student perceptions of teacher assessment or grading practices that could be used in a short-cycle continuous improvement process. Besides the existing

PERTS focus on student perceptions of receiving useful feedback, it is also important to gauge students' experiences of existing grading practices, as prior research has documented the tendency of students who receive failing grades with no opportunity for retakes or resubmissions to lose hope and stop trying. It is also crucial to measure the extent to which students have an accurate understanding of how they are performing in a class and how grading practices are affecting their effort.

In addition, we share some specific survey items in the appendix that measure students' perceptions of their parents' involvement in their education. We have used these items in previous research, and have evidence that they can show the hypothesized difference between involvement levels of students' parents in eighth grade as compared to ninth grade. Those engaged in improvement efforts to address the frequently observed decline in parental involvement as students transition to high school could make use of these measures as they seek to improve the ways high schools engage their families.[14] Given the well-documented low response rates to district surveys of families and the likelihood of a biased sample, using student survey results to measure family engagement is a promising measurement alternative for continuous improvement efforts.[15]

CONCLUDING THOUGHTS

You may still be skeptical about the possibility of measuring what is critical in the improvement effort you envision. It is true that important things are often difficult to measure, and we often fall prey to the temptation to search under the streetlight because that is where the light is, to paraphrase an old statistics joke. Given that instructional quality has been shown to be one of the most important determinants of student learning and student outcomes, and the more objective measures may be too cost-prohibitive to obtain, can we engage in continuous improvement efforts related to instruction in a scalable way? Is it possible to engage in continuous improvement efforts around family engagement if it is so difficult to obtain representative parent survey data frequently enough to inform a short-cycle process? What we have suggested in this chapter is that there are "good enough" alternative measures that are possible to collect with the resources available. Interim outcome measures on attendance and course grades are collected through standard work processes and can generally be easily accessed. Other process measures are often generated automatically or can be obtained readily. Brief student surveys collected electronically can be a doable way of measuring what students are experiencing. Using existing survey instruments and already developed items will facilitate the measurement process (see appendix, page 137). And networks of creative practitioners and researchers are continuing to work on this very issue.[16]

CHAPTER 5

How Can We Use "Disciplined Inquiry to Drive Improvement" in High School Outcomes?

Our goal in this chapter is to help our readers become more fluent in applying the disciplined inquiry process in their continuous improvement efforts around high school outcomes. As we begin, it is important to recall the questions Bryk and colleagues urge those engaged in continuous improvement efforts to ask themselves:

- "What specifically are we trying to accomplish?"
- "What change might we introduce and why?"
- "How will we know that a change is actually an improvement?"[1]

In this chapter we will model a process of responding to these questions and conducting disciplined inquiry for each of the five large change idea umbrellas we introduced in chapter 3: early warning systems, family engagement strategies, school connectedness, social-emotional learning, and instructional practice change.

To identify and focus in on a particular change idea within one of these broad umbrellas, we need to become more specific about our improvement goals. In particular, based on our analysis of the systems and subsystems within the school organization, we need to identify components of particular work processes where a specific change or set of changes has the potential to lead to better outcomes (and to outcomes that are linked to the student outcomes we seek to improve). As we discussed in chapter 4, we also need to consider how we will measure the results of our change efforts so we can determine whether they have actually resulted in improvement.

IMPROVING EARLY WARNING SYSTEMS

As we noted in chapter 3, early warning and intervention systems have become a widely implemented approach to improving student graduation outcomes in response to research findings from the mid-2000s. But there is considerable variation across schools in how well such systems are implemented and produce improved student results. As a nationally representative survey of high schools recently indicated, less than half the high schools claiming to have an early warning system (EWS) had "frequently coordinated" that system with services and strategies within the school to help struggling students.[2] Although there is growing evidence of the effectiveness of early warning systems in reducing problems in attendance, behavior, and course failure, analyses of EWS implementation challenges indicate the need for focused attention to improving their functioning.[3] It is important to consider how to improve the working of such systems so that they will reliably yield improved student outcomes. In this section we focus on three of the issues that have emerged as major challenges in the study of early warning systems. Given the difficulties schools have encountered in acquiring data in a timely way, the first is related to the actual data acquisition and manipulation process necessary to the smooth functioning of an early warning system. The second is ensuring that teams record data on the interventions they implement with students who manifest early warning indicators. The third is ensuring that teams systematically reflect on how those interventions have worked and use that process to inform follow-up interventions with students.

Improving the Indicator Data Acquisition and Manipulation Process

Since our early work in introducing the idea of early warning systems, the market has responded with a plethora of early warning tools and data systems for sale.[4] Systems that use predictive analytics have gone so far as to assign students a graduation probability score (that can change daily), based on metrics that combine the different warning indicators in particular ways. Districts have made a wide variety of decisions regarding data systems and tools, and our first step in working with schools has often been focused on deciding how best to structure the data and data monitoring process within the existing context. This may mean simplifying a complex early warning system to make the data usable within a continuous improvement framework.

What are we trying to accomplish? If our ultimate goal is to keep students on track to graduation, they need to earn their course credits on time. Increasing the percentage of students who pass courses and earn credit is a critical improvement goal. Schools would set specific goals based on their own context. For example, if 20 percent of students are failing to earn credit for at least one course, the school team might agree on a goal of reducing that percentage to 15 percent this year, 10 percent next year, 5 percent the following year, and less than 5 percent by the fourth year. But to accomplish this goal, the school also needs to set specific goals related to the process of monitoring and intervening with students at risk of failing their courses. The first or second quarterly grade is highly predictive of the final grade, and so close monitoring and intervention after Quarter 1 failure is a crucial interim step.

What change might we introduce, and why? As we consider the steps in the process needed to ensure these interventions, it is clear that the data system must be organized to create a list of students with failing grades at Quarter 1 (by grade level and subject or course) that can be used to guide the outreach and intervention efforts. In schools where producing and using a list of students with Q1 failing grades is not a typical work process, we recommend implementing this process. This would mean determining the steps involved in generating such a list from the school or district data system and making the list part of the specific responsibilities of a particular staff member or team. (Many schools already generate a so-called D/E list regularly from online gradebook data, even before the end of the quarterly marking period, but we include this first step for those schools that may still need to make this a standard work process. We focus on standard work processes and data collection around interventions related to Q1 failure in the next section.)

How will we know that the change is an improvement? Although the ultimate improvement we are seeking is a reduction in course failure (or an increase in earned course credits), one can measure improvement in the interim steps and stages. Generation of the list for the first time, or at an earlier date than has been accomplished in the past, or organized in useful new ways (by teacher, subject, grade level, etc.) represents an improvement in the school's standard work processes. Measuring improvement in this preliminary step is more qualitative and less precise than measuring other steps in the process. We dive more deeply into the improvement cycle of inquiry process as we discuss the monitoring and intervention process, and particularly the data collection and analysis process related to interventions.

Improving the Data Collection and Analysis Process

What are we trying to accomplish? As a step toward the ultimate aim of reducing course failure, one could set the specific aim of ensuring the following interventions for each student receiving a failing grade on the first quarter report card: receive a "check-in for improvement" conversation within two weeks of the Q1 report card with a teacher, counselor, or administrator to establish a plan for turning the failing grade around; and receive a follow-up conversation at least four weeks prior to the end of the semester to discuss progress and whether additional steps need to be taken to ensure the student will receive a passing grade. Crucial steps in this process include assignment of responsibility to staff members for discussing the list, selecting the best person to have a conversation with the student on how to improve the grade (based on the particular circumstances and who has a positive relationship with the student), and implementing interventions for students. It is also critical to determine a process for documenting whether or not these steps occurred (including the addition of specific information about these improvement conversations in a file that can be used by school staff throughout the year).

What change might we introduce, and why? Depending on the work processes already in place at the school, the aim of accomplishing these conversations with students may be part of the change. If the plan for these check-in conversations is already in place, the process of documenting them systematically may be the change needed in standard work processes.

How will we know that the change is an improvement? If systematic records about conversations with students receiving failing grades at Q1 have not been kept in the past, the evidence of record-keeping (in a digital file that can be shared and manipulated for analysis) is a simple qualitative measure of improvement. When record-keeping becomes a standard work process, one can measure improvement in the percentage of students receiving check-in conversations, as well as in the percentage of students with specific information about those check-ins in the records.

An Example Plan-Do-Study-Act Cycle of Inquiry for Q1 Failing Grade Conversations

How can a school team conduct disciplined inquiry around the improvement process for monitoring and intervening with students who have failing grades at Q1? In the following section we provide an example of how teams could engage in each of the Plan, Do, Study, and Act components of such a cycle of inquiry.

Plan. The planning process for implementing the proposed change would need to focus primarily on outlining all the necessary steps and identifying who is responsible for accomplishing them. Assuming that all the necessary data has been generated in a timely way, the team assigned to accomplishing and documenting the check-in improvement conversations with students needs to begin with a concrete estimate of the size of the task as it begins planning. How many students typically have failing Q1 grades? (If this information has not been collected in the past, the team will need to anticipate more planning time once the lists have been generated.) How many school staff are needed to conduct the check-ins, and how will staff be matched to specific students? Where will the datafile documenting the conversations reside, and how will data be entered (for example, by individual staff or by a central datamaster receiving documentation from individual staff)? What is needed to help staff meet the timeframe goal for the check-in conversations so that students have sufficient time to begin turning things around in the courses where they are struggling? Is there a need to schedule team meetings during the intervention process for support and any needed midterm corrections, as well as after the end of the second quarter for group reflection?

Do. The most labor-intensive part of the process is actually doing the improvement conversation interventions and documenting them. As staff conduct the conversations and data are entered documenting them, it would be useful for all staff to jot down (in electronic files) any issues that they may notice about the process so that they can reflect productively about those issues as a group. What barriers do staff encounter in seeking to check in with students? What interferes with documenting interventions as data? Collecting these observations in a systematic way is a different sort of data collection that may need to become part of standard work processes, as it is a critical component of evaluating the process of the intervention and identifying additional needs for changes in how work is conducted.

Study. When the team meets at the end of the second quarter (after Q2 grades have been recorded), there will be several types of data to analyze and results to discuss. The team might begin by analyzing their qualitative notes about the process. What seemed to work well? What were the barriers or factors that interfered with making progress? The Study component of the process also needs to focus intently on the data regarding the intervention—conversations with each of the students receiving failing grades in Q1. What percentage of students on the Q1 failures list have documentation of intervention? Were there interventions that did not get documented? Why? What details about those conversations were recorded? Were additional needs (for tutoring, counseling follow-up, possible social worker intervention, etc.) identified and recorded? What evidence is there that additional interventions occurred for those students? What patterns can be detected in the data (by demographic group, person responsible for interventions, or other groupings) that could be relevant?

The team also needs to examine the student outcome data in comparison with past trends (or another appropriate comparison group). What percentage of students with failing grades in Q1 successfully recovered in Q2? How does this compare with the prior year's data on Q2 failure (if available)? Did additional failures occur in other courses students were passing at Q1? Is there any discernable pattern or relationship between documented interventions and students' Q2 grades? Do the interventions seem to be making any difference? Besides analysis of the data on students with Q1 failures, the team will also need to consider how many students received failing grades for the first time in Q2, and how those results should influence the work of the team going forward. For example, if a significant number of students with Ds in Q1 went on to fail in Q2, the team should consider how viable it would be to plan for including students with D grades on the intervention list.

Act. Based on their analyses of the data and conclusions drawn from the Study part of the inquiry cycle, the team then makes decisions about how to proceed in the future. Was the intervention within the current capacity of school to implement? If so, did it have enough impact that it should become part of the school's standard work process for responding to Q1 course failures? Or was the impact not worth the effort required? Do additional improvement ideas need to be developed and tested? Did the change idea intervention work for some types of students or under certain circumstances more than others? If so, are different or more intensive interventions needed in some cases? How will documentation and subsequent discussion around more intensive kinds of interventions be ensured?

One can see how this same cycle of inquiry could be applied to more intensive interventions that a team may recommend for particular students. For example, suppose the early warning team decides that certain struggling students need to receive regular tutoring. In our experience, teams often make these recommendations and may even follow up to ensure that students are attending tutoring, but the follow-through process of documenting these decisions and then circling back to evaluate how well the interventions are working for students often does not happen. The team might decide to focus a continuous improvement process on ensuring that these steps actually occur, and on analyzing the results to ascertain the extent to which the interventions are actually achieving their intended goal. Ultimately, the continuous improvement process around the early warning and intervention system also needs to analyze student outcome data at the end of the year to determine whether more students are succeeding in earning enough high school course credits to stay on track to graduation. Identifying points at which the monitoring process may be breaking down or interventions that don't seem to be working is critical to the improvement process. And as we shall discuss more in chapter 6, sharing experiences with teams from other schools that are also seeking to implement effective early warning and intervention systems is an important part of the process of learning to improve.

IMPROVING SCHOOLS' FAMILY ENGAGEMENT EFFORTS

As we discussed in chapter 3, research indicates that high schools typically do much less to reach out to the families of their students than do elementary and middle schools. Research has also found that high school efforts to communicate with families make a difference in parental support to students and to student outcomes. But a continuous improvement effort needs to be much more explicit about what it is seeking to accomplish than the vague "increasing family engagement" goals we typically find in school improvement plans. *We need to be more specific about what we are trying to accomplish.* We suggest a couple of specific family engagement related goals in the next section, together with detailed descriptions of a disciplined inquiry process for each.

Parent Portal Use

What are we trying to accomplish? Building on research findings about the positive impact school communications about the parent portal can have on both usage and student outcomes, we could set an improvement goal around increasing the number of families who are accessing the parent portal.[5] Although our ultimate goal is improved student outcomes, during the improvement process we have a more specific goal related to a particular lever we believe is related to that student outcome.

What change might we introduce, and why? One evidence-based change idea that we recommend involves sending families in the target population (such as all ninth grade families at the study school) specific communications about the usefulness of the parent portal and how to access it. This change idea comes from a prior study that found positive results in both family behaviors related to the portal and also in student course grade outcomes.

How will we know that the change is an improvement? This will require a systematic plan for identifying comparable groups of students and parents—one group to receive the intervention or change and the other to experience "business as usual." Then it will be necessary to conduct the rigorous comparison of parent portal usage in both groups to ascertain whether the difference is substantial enough to consider scaling up. We will need a good measurement of a specific change outcome, such as the number or percentage of families logging into the portal during a specific time frame. At the same time, it will also be important to assess the extent to which the intervention was sufficiently implemented to help explain possible outcomes, as failure to find a positive result could be due to poor implementation.

An Example Plan-Do-Study-Act Cycle of Inquiry for a Parent Portal Intervention

Disciplined inquiry around the improvement process for increasing the percentage of families accessing the parent portal could fit well into the typical short-cycle inquiry process.

Plan. Planning for the introduction of a change or intervention involves not only the specific details of the intervention itself, but also requires identification of intervention and comparison groups and of a data collection process. Planning for data collection also requires at least a preliminary plan regarding how data will be analyzed and what is needed to be able to draw reliable conclusions.

Identification of target group and comparison group If the continuous improvement team is school-based, it needs to decide whether it wants to conduct a schoolwide intervention or focus on one grade level. It could be good to begin with an outreach to just the ninth grade families. Finding an appropriate comparison group could be challenging. While random assignment of students' families from the same school's ninth grade cohort to a treatment or a comparison group might be methodologically appealing, it could potentially evoke resentment or result in contamination if information sent to the treatment group is shared with friends in the control group. Comparing the treatment group with students and families from the same school the prior year would be an alternative strategy if parent portal usage data from the prior year can be obtained easily. If there have been major changes over time that make such comparisons problematic, it may be better to make comparisons with a cohort of students and families at a similar high school in the district the same year.

Intervention details It is important to precisely specify the components of the change idea or intervention. In this example that involves communication to families, the key components can be organized within the familiar W questions: Who, What, When, Where, Why, and How (we will focus on the first three here).

Who. The Who question involves both who will receive the communication, and also who will perform all the necessary actions to ensure it is done. Once the target intervention group is selected (for example, ninth grade families), it is essential to ensure that contact information is available for all those involved. That would be one of the first activities for the Who group designated to perform all the necessary tasks.

What. Here we need to specify what exactly the steps in the intervention are. What is the message that families will receive? In what formats? (This may merge into the How and Where questions.) Family engagement experts emphasize how important it is to use multiple forms of communication, as using just one form generally does not adequately reach all families. Communicating more than once is also a critical component of effective family engagement (which merges into the When question). Identifying all the steps for making the communications happen is crucial: drafting and finalizing the message, formatting it for all communications platforms, executing steps for dissemination (including acquiring all the contact information, like email addresses, phone numbers, home addresses, etc.), and planning for responding to family questions or other communications in response to the school communications.

Following intervention practices that have been found to be effective in research studies, we recommend at the very least that messaging to families about the portal be conducted through a mailing to the home and followed up with a phone call.[6] To the extent that automatic technical structures are in place that do not require excessive staff time, it would also be useful to alert families through email and text messaging to expect the mailing (which gives them a relatively easy way to communicate back to the school with questions they may have).

We recommend that the content of the communications include the following:

- specific details about how the parent portal is useful for monitoring grades and helping ensure student success (explaining to families the Why question)
- encouragement to log into the portal at least biweekly if already connected

- instructions about calling the school for account information (including the school telephone number) as well as step-by-step instructions for using that information to access the portal
- an example portal screen shot with interpretations of the data contained there
- a link embedded into the email and/or text message to an online tutorial about using the portal system if the district has created such a tutorial (and include the website link address in the paper mailing as well)

When. To be most effective, this plan should be carried out at the very beginning of the school year (by the end of the first week of school, if possible). This plan is expected to increase the percentage of families logging into the portal system over the course of the first semester. Based on prior research, the plan is also expected to improve students' grade point averages and potentially reduce the percentage of students failing a course. This is expected to occur because of increased monitoring and intervention by parents.

Planning for data collection The data needed for disciplined inquiry include both process and outcome measures. Process measures have to do with how well the intervention was actually implemented. The outcome measures for this inquiry involve data on logins to the parent portal.

Checklists for the various steps of implementing the intervention can be used in the data collection process (e.g., spreadsheets documenting when particular steps were accomplished). It is also important to plan ahead to collect data regarding foreseeable issues. Because mailings often confront the challenge of old or incorrect addresses, there should be a plan to maintain data about returned mailings, corrected addresses, and execution of replacement mailings. Maintaining data on family calls to obtain portal account information is another important step in this data collection process if an efficient method can be implemented. It is important to recognize that school leaders are continually faced with challenges related to use of staff time, and so decisions about the precision of data collection must always be weighed against the opportunity costs related to other uses of staff time. When time and labor are in short supply, using student interns who are learning about working in the "real world" on such clerical tasks would appear to be a win-win solution if confidentiality requirements permit. One can meet both school needs and the need for students to have opportunities to gain experience on real workplace tasks or fulfill service-learning requirements.

The best outcome measure for a parent portal intervention would typically be a count of parent logins to the parent portal during a specific time frame. In our experience, the data collection process will probably be automatic, as portal systems generally keep a digital record of each parent login. It does take the time of district IT staff to download the data and link individual parent records to student administrative data to allow for analyses by subgroup characteristics. It will be necessary for school leaders to make the case for these data requests to the district office in advance of beginning such an intervention, as these data are not typically shared routinely in our experience.

Do. This step involves not only execution of the plan, but observation of how the plan is executed. What kind of issues arise in implementation? What feedback (if any) did the school receive from families about the feasibility of accessing the portal? What issues related to internet access were uncovered? Perhaps there were clarity issues in the instructions provided to families about using the portal. The Do stage is an opportunity to observe how the intervention is working and to note ways that implementation could be improved in the future.

Study. Besides analyses of the implementation data described above, this step requires timely data from the district about the number and percentage of families accessing the portal system and frequency of access. The inquiry process requires not only data for the study school over the course of the semester (perhaps monthly), but also comparison group data. Ideally, the comparison group would be a demographically and academically similar school not involved in the intervention. In addition, it would be useful to compare study school results to the portal use rate for the study school's prior year cohort at the same time of the year (including the same prior data for the comparison school if possible). Did the intervention result in increased portal usage for the study school? The study step of the inquiry process would also involve comparison of course failure rates for Semester 1 from the previous year and current year for both the study school and comparison school. Was there a decline in course failure rates (or increase in the mean grade point average) at the study school (or improvement relative to the comparison school)? How might implementation findings (e.g., low rates of families calling the school for account information) help to explain outcome findings? Could better implementation help to improve the outcomes of the intervention?

Act. Based on the findings from the Study component of the inquiry cycle, the continuous improvement team must now make decisions about next steps. Another trial could be warranted if implementation issues are uncovered and it is possible to improve how the intervention is rolled out in a subsequent trial. If intervention appeared to occur smoothly but no improvements in logins to the portal system were evident, the team might have to reconsider whether another trial of the intervention would be useful or whether they should search for a new improvement idea to test. We often learn as much from failure as from success, so improvement teams need to be aware that failure is an inevitable and important part of the continuous improvement process. It is not a signal that the effort was wasted. It is part of the process. It may advance our understanding of how to solve the problem we are addressing as much as—and sometimes more than—an initial success.

Parent Texting Intervention

The parent portal provides information about assignments and tests after the fact. But as research has shown and some teachers have concluded, it is often useful for families to have information about when tests are occurring so they can encourage their teens to study and prepare.[7] (Like us, you may have experience as a parent about this.) Based on the research evidence, reminders to parents or families by text about when assessments and assignments are occurring are likely to help more students be successful the first time in earning their ninth grade credits.[8]

What are we trying to accomplish? Again, we are trying to increase course passing rates (credit accrual), particularly among ninth graders. In introducing the text messaging change idea, we are seeking to increase parent information about course assessments and assignments in order to encourage more informed parental support at critical times for student course performance, with the hypothesis that this will improve student outcomes.

What could disciplined inquiry around the results of implementing such a change idea involve? We will not repeat all the details of a Plan-Do-Study-Act cycle, but provide some overarching suggestions below.

Plan. Given that this texting practice is an additional step for teachers beyond their responsibility to regularly update the online gradebook that feeds the parent portal, this intervention idea needs a few willing early adopters or testers among the faculty who are willing to try it out, analyze the data and study the results, and share their findings with their colleagues. Planning for the intervention involves addressing several issues. There are numerous logistical details (among others: obtaining parent phone numbers and permission to receive text messages, finding a texting platform that can automate the process to make it doable for high school teachers with busy schedules, setting up a schedule for texting, scripting the messages about upcoming tests and assignments). In addition, it is essential to identify a baseline or comparison group for analyses to determine whether the intervention resulted in improved student grades.

Do. Then the teachers need to execute the plan. As they do, they should keep track of any barriers encountered (wrong numbers, complaints from parents, etc.) to discuss during the next stage of the cycle. Data collection on student performance continues as usual.

Study. After the intervention cycle has been completed (after a quarter, or perhaps a semester, depending on the school and classroom context), the group of teachers conducting this improvement effort needs to analyze student performance results (against an appropriate comparison group) to see if the intervention made a difference. This could go beyond simple analysis of changes in percentage of students receiving a passing grade to include changes in other measures (e.g., percentage of assignments submitted, average report card grade, etc.) It is also crucial to discuss the data on implementation issues to understand how they may have affected outcomes or how barriers identified may affect the usefulness of this intervention.

Act. Based on the results, teachers may want to share their findings and encourage broader implementation of the change idea, assuming they find the same positive results that researchers have reported. They may encounter resistance from colleagues, given the additional work involved in communicating with families. Other resistance may come from those who believe such interventions diminish student responsibility and independence. Sharing analyses of the extent to which such interventions address equity issues and succeed in narrowing gaps between groups in student outcomes may help to address faculty resistance.

INCREASING SCHOOL CONNECTEDNESS

Relationships matter for learning. As we pointed out in chapter 3, a large body of research emphasizes the importance of both teacher-student and student-to-student relationships in improving learning outcomes. Feeling you belong and are part of a community makes school a place you want to be. Knowing that someone cares and is advocating actively for your success makes all the difference. In this section we consider what disciplined inquiry around the implementation and impact of two potential change ideas for strengthening school connectedness could look like: increasing positive relationships through regular greeting of students by teachers, and intentional outreach to students to connect them with extracurricular activities.

Increasing Belongingness and School Connectedness Through Positive Adult Interactions

What are we trying to accomplish? In this example, we focus on whether two measures of school connectedness—attendance rate and perception of teacher caring—can be positively affected by a change in teacher practices regarding interactions with students. We are ultimately interested in whether this change will also have a positive effect on student course performance (measured by course passing).

What change might we introduce, and why? The change we propose builds on evidence of a positive effect on behavior and student engagement of the practice of teachers greeting middle school students at the classroom door.[9] Could this positive effect also occur for ninth grade students in high school?

An Example Plan-Do-Study-Act Cycle of Inquiry for Increasing School Connectedness Through Positive Greeting Practices

Plan. Planning for an intervention designed to increase positive greeting interactions by teachers would probably need to begin with agreement on the specific practices to be implemented. To what extent does the improvement team want to use the exact evidence-based practices described in the research article and to what extent should the team adapt them for their own context?[10] In particular, in addition to the positive greeting of students by name at the classroom door, the intervention with positive effects included the following components: "Teachers deliver preplanned, precorrective statements to increase the likelihood of students transitioning successfully into the classroom and engaging as quickly as possible in the planned learning activity . . . . [and] strategically provide behavior-specific praise statements to reinforce desired behavior and capitalize on social learning."[11] The improvement team may or may not decide to include all these components, or could potentially substitute others. It is important that the team consider how the planned intervention will differ from routine conditions. (If such greetings are already a common occurrence in the school, this intervention is probably not the one to be considered.)

Planning for the intervention and data collection would require steps we have outlined in other examples above (selection of treatment and comparison groups, time duration of the implementation, data collection around implementation issues and outcome measures). We will not repeat details about all these steps here, though introduction of the intervention at the beginning of Q2 would offer a good baseline comparison group from Q1 (in addition to another comparison group not receiving the intervention at all). The team would need to plan the logistics of collecting pre- and postintervention student survey measures of "teacher caring" (from the PERTS survey described in chapter 4).[12] Such a survey might also include a specific question related to the greeting intervention to measure implementation. Depending on the district data system, less planning would be needed around collecting attendance and course performance data. If teachers are willing to plan to spend the time daily to complete mini surveys (two to three questions) about their implementation of the practice(s) and their rating of classroom management problems encountered that day, such data would also be useful, but student survey reports at the end of the intervention period might be a more feasible method of data collection.

Do. The key component of this part of the process, besides implementing the intervention itself, is actual completion of the data collection process around implementation and immediate effects observed in the classroom, as well as the pre- and postsurvey data collection. Creation of an automated google doc tool would facilitate data analysis if teachers are able to reliably enter data electronically each day. Similarly, electronic student survey data collection will also make analysis much more feasible.

Study. As discussed earlier, it is essential to analyze the extent to which the intervention was conducted as planned before drawing conclusions about its effectiveness. Then an analysis of change in student perceptions of "teacher caring" and attendance and course grade outcomes would be appropriate.

Act. Based on conclusions from the data analysis, the team would decide whether it seems worthwhile to keep the intervention, adapt it in a future cycle, or pursue alternative directions. If evidence is lacking for a positive impact on student outcomes, it is important that the team consider implementation issues that could be corrected before jettisoning the idea completely.

Increasing School Connectedness Through Extracurricular Activities

What are we trying to accomplish? In this example, we continue to be focused on increasing the percentage of students who successfully earn their high school course credits. Our inquiry examines whether specific changes in school practices can lead to increased student participation in extracurricular activities, and whether this in turn is related to improved student engagement in school (measured by attendance) and improved student performance in courses (measured by course passing).

What change might we introduce, and why? Building on the evidence-based change idea of "checking and connecting" with students who are absent, we suggest an additional step related to inquiring about students' interests and how they are participating in extracurricular activities.[13] These check and connect discussions could then include encouragement to become actively involved in an activity of particular interest or to help start a particular affinity or interest group. Follow-up with these students (and all additional students receiving a failing grade at the end of Q1) would then include continued encouragement regarding extracurriculars. Activities that give students a sense of accomplishment and satisfaction in being able to help others are particularly beneficial.

An Example Plan-Do-Study-Act Cycle of Inquiry for Increasing School Connectedness Through Student Participation in Extracurriculars

Plan. A team might productively begin a disciplined inquiry process for an intervention designed to increase school connectedness through participation in extracurricular activities with an informal needs assessment, such as through conversations with school personnel about the extent to which struggling students are also disconnected from other school activities. Such conversations should also explore systemic issues that could be raising barriers (policies around GPA requirements for school sports, transportation issues that could prevent students from staying after school, etc.). It will be important to address such barriers to participating in extracurricular activities.

This change idea builds on the assumption that the school has an existing organizational routine or standard work process for "checking and connecting" with students who have a certain number of absences. If this is not the case, the team should begin by assessing the extent of attendance problems and establishing a process by which all students missing, for example, 10 percent of school days receive a positive interaction with a caring adult to explore reasons for the absences and strategies for more regular attendance. Assuming that such a routine is in place, the team would plan for how to ensure that these interactions also include a question about the student's interest in at least one extracurricular activity and active encouragement to help the student become involved in an activity of interest. Planning for how to ensure that follow-up conversations with each student are conducted is also crucial. The team should consider the same types of issues discussed earlier for other change ideas regarding identification of a target intervention group and similar comparison group and data collection issues.

For this initiative, the key data collection issue would involve planning a process for recording data on whether or not absent students had a conversation with an adult at the school about extracurricular activities, whether a follow-up conversation occurred sometime during the inquiry period (typically a school quarter), and whether the student is actually participating in an extracurricular activity. Again, it would be helpful for members of the intervention team to plan to record their observations about implementation issues over the course of the inquiry period. The relevant outcome data (student attendance rates) are probably routinely recorded in digital files and would not require additional planning.

Do. The team would then execute the plan for intervention and data collection during the inquiry period.

Study. After the inquiry period the team would first analyze the implementation data. How many of the absent students received check-in conversations, and how many of those also included a discussion about extracurriculars? What did data on follow-up conversations indicate about the extent to which it was possible to successfully implement the intervention? What barriers were encountered, and how could they be addressed? It may be necessary to discuss how to add other extracurricular activities to help meet the needs and interests of students. If the intervention was successfully implemented, is there evidence that it had a positive impact on increased extracurricular participation, student attendance, and course performance?

Act. Based on findings from their disciplined inquiry, the team would then decide whether to continue the intervention or adapt it in some way. The team would also consider whether there was sufficient positive evidence to scale such an intervention to affect greater numbers of students.

INCREASING OPPORTUNITIES FOR SOCIAL-EMOTIONAL LEARNING

As we noted in chapter 3, there has been considerable recent research around the effectiveness of social-emotional learning interventions. Student mindsets and noncognitive orientations and skills matter for academic performance. In this section we focus on two research-based interventions that appear promising for changing students' orientations in ways that will improve academic outcomes: a growth mindset and a sense of purpose.[14] Focusing on a growth mindset has played an important role in the learning process for at least one group of high schools actively engaged in continuous improvement.[15]

Growth Mindset

There has been widespread discussion for more than a decade about the importance of helping students to view their abilities as malleable, something that can grow over time as they exert effort.[16] Students with a growth mindset are more likely to exert effort and thus more likely to have positive academic outcomes.[17] Positive research findings about the impact of short interventions designed to increase growth mindset are growing in number.

What are we trying to accomplish? We continue our focus on increasing the percentage of students who successfully earn their high school course credits. This inquiry examines whether student mindsets can be shifted in specific ways that can lead to increased effort and improved academic outcomes (measured by student course grades).

What change might we introduce, and why? If growth mindset interventions have not already been conducted at the middle grades level, it is likely that such an intervention could be useful in helping ninth graders view themselves as able to grow in mastery through concerted effort. The team might want to select an already-developed growth mindset intervention to use with their students. Projects for Education Research That Scales (PERTS) has a freely available "Growth Mindset for Ninth Graders" set of two thirty-minute modules that the team might introduce in a cycle of inquiry.[18] PERTS can also provide valuable assistance to schools around such an inquiry. They provide not only access to the online intervention for students, but also data collection, analysis, and reporting to the school team around the change in student growth mindset levels. We outline additional steps in the inquiry process that would be important for school teams to take below.

An Example Plan-Do-Study-Act Cycle of Inquiry for a Growth Mindset Intervention

Plan. As noted above, the team planning for this disciplined inquiry would have investigated whether students had received any growth mindset interventions already during the middle grades. The team would also need to conduct inquiries into participation in the PERTS growth mindset research. PERTS provides a detailed information packet and checklist regarding this planning for implementation.[19] This includes ensuring sufficient computer availability and internet access as well as scheduling for the survey administration and student participation in the online modules (including multiple survey administrations over a one- to four-week period). It also includes decisions about which ninth grade students or classrooms will participate. The PERTS platform collects pre- and postintervention student survey data on growth mindset before and after the intervention is delivered through the online platform. It is important to note that the PERTS platform does not support a continuous improvement inquiry using a comparison group during the same time period, and it may not even be possible to use the same PERTS survey items measuring growth mindset with students not participating in the intervention. Using the PERTS platform would involve some tradeoff between increased ease of implementing the intervention and the rigor of the disciplined inquiry around it (though it would still be possible to compare course performance data from the intervention cohort with that of the previous year's cohort). Depending on the time and human capital resources available, a school may have to choose between using the PERTS platform and not conducting an intervention at all. The improvement team could potentially plan to try out the PERTS platform and use the inquiry process to evaluate whether or not to continue using it. It will be important for the team to plan for data collection around implementation issues (similar to the process outlined in examples above) and their assessments of the online intervention itself.

Do. With careful planning, implementation should proceed smoothly. In this example, most data collection is automatic (by PERTS and the school's online gradebook system) but the team needs to ensure that some sort of systematic data collection (such as weekly notes) occurs around implementation issues.

Study. Besides studying the results of growth mindset change from the survey results provided by PERTS, the team will also want to examine the extent to which academic outcomes improved (compared to a previous cohort). As noted above, this may not be as rigorous an inquiry as one might like, as one may not be able to attribute improvement in academic outcomes to the mindset intervention if any other factors have changed. But the inquiry may provide useful findings as part of a larger improvement process.

Act. Because this particular PERTS intervention is only for ninth graders, the team's decision about next steps would focus primarily on whether to continue participation the following year and how early in the year to schedule the intervention. The team may also want to consider other ways besides the PERTS intervention to increase students' growth mindset. There may be ways to improve the effectiveness of a growth mindset intervention in particular contexts, as one research team using a design thinking approach has recently demonstrated.[20] The team may also want to explore how teacher professional development could help increase the ways that teachers encourage a growth mindset in their classroom interactions with students.[21]

Sense of Purpose

What are we trying to accomplish? We continue our focus on increasing the percentage of students who successfully earn their high school course credits. This inquiry examines whether particular interventions can shift student mindsets in specific ways that can lead to increased effort and improved academic outcomes. Specifically, we examine in this example whether an intervention to give students a transcendent sense of purpose for learning can improve student engagement in school (measured by attendance) and improve student performance in courses (measured by course passing).

What change might we introduce, and why? Given that sense of purpose has been shown to be strongly related to academic performance and that interventions can increase this sense of purpose, it is reasonable to expect a positive result from a short intervention designed to increase students' sense of purpose in learning.[22] The sense of purpose intervention conducted by researchers had several components.[23] Relying on previous research findings, they deliberately did not try to tell students what their purposes should be, but used a more indirect approach that suggested that students like themselves had a transcendent purpose for learning so they could make the world a better place. The intervention involved:

- asking students to write a short essay response to a prompt about social injustice issues;
- presenting students with survey evidence about other students' motives for learning that included pro-social goals about making a positive difference in the world;

- reading a quotation from a student in the study they were discussing with intervention students that emphasized pro-social goals for learning; and
- having students write their own message to fellow students about their reasons for learning.[24]

This took roughly an hour to conduct.

An Example Plan-Do-Study-Act Cycle of Inquiry for a Sense of Purpose Intervention

Plan. The planning of the intervention is more intensive in this example than in the growth mindset example. The team may want to consider how to adapt the intervention described above to their own context. They will need to plan an implementation timeline (even if they simply use the hour-long version of the intervention). One could envision a scenario in which it is included in a suite of social-emotional learning and community-building activities during the first week or two of school that are integrated with rigorous and engaging learning activities related to high-interest issues for students. Again, the team will need to plan for how meaningful comparisons can be made between the intervention group and a similar comparison group. (Will only some students in a particular year receive the intervention so that comparisons can be made with a group in the same cohort?) In addition to examining course grades, the team may want to plan to collect student survey data using the "meaningful work" measures from PERTS as well as data about how implementation proceeded.[25]

Do. If planning was sufficient, implementation should proceed smoothly. Again, making sure that data are collected during this stage is crucial.

Study and Act. As noted earlier, analysis of how the implementation process proceeded is a critical part of the inquiry process, together with analysis of outcome data. Based on analysis of student outcome data (course grades), the team should be able to ascertain whether the intervention made a difference and whether or not it makes sense to continue the particular intervention with other groups of students. The team might also consider how teachers could continue to encourage this sense of purpose for learning within their students through their everyday classroom experiences.

IMPROVING INSTRUCTIONAL PRACTICES

As indicated in our root cause analysis and fishbone diagram in chapter 3, student failure can be linked to different types of instructional practices. One reason why students do not earn passing grades in their high school courses is that they find the work boring and unmeaningful or do not see how it is linked to their future, and hence see no reason to exert the effort needed to complete the work required of them. Although unengaging instruction is not necessarily the only (or even the primary) cause of student failure, there is substantial evidence that certain instructional practices, like providing choices to students, can help to increase student engagement and motivation to engage in learning.[26] Another reason why students may shut down and not put forth effort in their classes is their lack of confidence in their ability to make sufficient progress to make a difference in their grades. Adjusting the instructional practice of grading to allow students to improve their work and increase their mastery also has the potential to lead to improved student performance. In the following section we outline a couple of examples of how school teams could engage in disciplined inquiry around particular changes in instructional practices.

Increasing Student Choices and Sense of Autonomy

What are we trying to accomplish? In this scenario, we have already identified a problem with a significant number of students failing to complete multiple assignments (either classwork or homework), resulting in low or failing course grades. We are seeking to increase students' successful completion of course assignments, a leading indicator of course grades and course passing rates. In particular, we are focused on learning whether specific changes in instructional practice can lead to greater student motivation and effort to complete work.

What change might we introduce, and why? Research evidence has identified autonomy as a key factor in student motivation and suggests that students respond positively to opportunities for choice with increased interest, motivation, and effort.[27] So the change we might introduce revolves around providing increased choice to students in their class and homework assignments.

How will we know that the change is an improvement? To address this, we need to consider the measures we might use to assess the change in outcomes after introducing a change idea. We would recommend at least two different types of measurement of improvement here. First, it is important to measure student perceptions of whether the change led to an experience of increased choice, and the extent to which students experienced this as a positive change. Second, we need to measure whether there was an actual difference in the percentage of completed assignments and/or the percentage of students completing all assignments, and whether this made a difference in students' grades.

An Example Plan-Do-Study-Act Cycle of Inquiry for a Student Choice in Assignments Intervention

In this section we share suggestions about how to implement a disciplined inquiry process for an intervention designed to increase students' choices and thereby their motivation to exert the effort to complete assignments.

Plan. As we noted earlier, the planning stage for a cycle of inquiry requires attention to not only the intervention itself, but also to the selection of intervention and comparison groups as well as planning for data collection (including baseline data before the start of the intervention).

In this scenario, three English teachers at the high school are willing to work together as a group to try out a change related to increased student choice and investigate its effect on student attitudes and effort, ultimately measured by assignment completion. The comparison group they may identify for the first stages of this improvement effort could be their previous year's students (assuming there has been no systematic change in the characteristics of students or the particular courses they are teaching). Although it is theoretically possible for teachers to introduce the change idea for one class and not a comparable second class, it is probably better to avoid a situation in which students in different classes with the same teacher during the same semester may compare notes and complain about this differential treatment.

Let's assume, for the sake of argument, that these three teachers had offered little if any choice on particular assignments in the previous year. In designing the intervention, the group might decide to begin the semester for a week or two with this same approach, and plan to introduce the change to students at the beginning of week three or four. (This allows for baseline survey data collection from students about their experience of choice at the very beginning of the course that can be compared with end-of-course survey data.) The specific details of the intervention could vary, depending on how many assignments involve choices and what types of choices. For example, if there is a short daily "do now" type exercise, there could be two or three different versions among which students could choose. Or the teachers could plan to offer two or three different choices for class and homework assignments at least once a week, if daily choices are simply too overwhelming for the teacher to implement given planning time available. Teachers could even offer choices among different types of assessments (testing, papers, projects, presentations, etc.). We provide examples of various choices of tools for "assessment that motivates" on our website.[28] Developing these choices could be distributed among the teachers on the improvement team, potentially lightening the load as they share their plans with one another. The planning process for the intervention would need to result in a specific intervention plan linked to the course schedule and syllabus. For example, one could identify a particular number of assignments for which choices would be offered, and then plan the "menu" of choices (with specific assignment directions) for each of these assignments, together with some type of rubric for how the assignments will be assessed. (This plan could also be combined with a plan for choices on the daily "do now" exercises at the beginning of class, depending on how extensive a change effort one wanted to implement as a starting point.)

This approach obviously requires support from school and district leaders in contexts where curricula are explicitly prescribed. In our years in the field we recall district-mandated curricula with such specifically prescribed assignments (such as types of essays to prepare students for state-mandated testing) that teachers spoke of having to "go rogue" in their attempts to connect with their students and provide the motivation context for students to exert effort. Addressing a systemic problem that constrains teacher and student choice would need to occur prior to launching the type of change idea and associated improvement cycles proposed here.

Do. In this stage, the team executes the plan they have developed, and makes observations (collects data) on how things are going. Even with good planning, unforeseen issues are sure to arise. Keeping track of these issues (in a running journal and in regular discussions among the team members) is an important part of the observation process during the Do stage.

Study. At the end of the quarter the team can then study the results of the intervention. Was there an increase in students' perception of choice, and in their reported engagement with assignments, based on survey response data? Was there an increase in completed assignments, compared to the cohort from the previous year? Was there an improvement in student grades (and a decrease in failing quarter grades)? To what extent were there implementation challenges? How did the time costs of implementation compare with the benefits achieved?

Act. Based on the results of the Study phase, the team would then make decisions about whether to continue the intervention as it is, to adapt it in some ways, or to move in another change direction if there appears to be little chance this approach will lead to improvement. Again, such decisions will undoubtedly be informed by perceptions of whether the benefits of such an approach in increased student engagement are likely to justify the time costs for implementation.

Providing Students with Opportunities to Set Mastery Goals and Improve Their Work

Another root cause of student failure that we identified in chapter 3 was the tendency for students to give up, particularly when assessment systems make it difficult for students to succeed in passing a course after a certain point. Grading systems that average all grades together and provide few if any opportunities for students to relearn and redo substandard work exacerbate students' inclinations to simply give up at a certain point.

What are we trying to accomplish? In this example, we continue to be focused on increasing the percentage of students who successfully earn their high school course credits, as well as increasing their mastery of skills they will need for postsecondary success. We are particularly focused on learning whether specific changes in instructional practices around assessment and grading can lead to higher rates of student mastery and successful course completion.

What change might we introduce, and why? One evidence-based change idea that deserves greater attention than it has received thus far involves helping students to set specific goals for mastering course content as a means of improving their academic performance.[29] This needs to go beyond vague goals of "improving my grades" or even "spending more time studying." Applying this change idea in foreign language classrooms involved a range of specific mastery goals (for example, the ability to engage in specific daily activities, such as ordering a meal at a restaurant, buying a ticket, etc.) as well as an action plan of how to achieve those goals. Evidence that this practice of setting mastery goals (with action plans to achieve them) was associated with higher achievement makes this a promising idea to try out in a continuous improvement effort at a high school. Evidence from one classroom and then a group of classrooms at their own school is likely to be more convincing to teachers to buy into such an improvement effort than evidence from academic research studies conducted elsewhere.

High school math teacher Matt Townsley recounts the story of how his personal experiment in transforming his grading practices to reflect standards-based or mastery principles spread to a small study group of colleagues in his own school and eventually districtwide.[30] It began with his questioning the widespread practice of grading that penalizes students with lower early homework and assessment grades. If those same students go on to show their mastery by the end of the course, he wondered why they should be treated differently, as systems that average all grades together tend to do. Not all teachers share this same philosophy, as we were quick to learn when leading professional development sessions about grading. Some teachers vigorously assert that students who "get it" earlier should be rewarded. Others who oppose giving students opportunities to retest and improve their grades stress that we need to prepare students for the real world where "you only have one shot at things, so you'd better get it right the first time."[31] (Whether or not this is actually true is a matter of debate.) Other teachers may not share that philosophical orientation about rewarding learning speed to the same extent, but definitely do not want to be bothered with the extra work of allowing students to redo assessments. Finding ways to make this mastery approach to learning a practical dimension of everyday work processes in teachers' lives is crucial for moving in this direction.[32]

How will we know that the change is an improvement? Again, we need to identify a comparison group and consider the measurement question to be able to assess whether change leads to improvement. And we would reiterate that at least two different types of measurement would be useful. Measuring student perceptions will help us to understand the mechanism through which changes in assessment practices may be leading to changes in student performance and outcomes. (We provide some potential survey measures in the appendix.) As in the previous example, we again would need to measure whether there was an actual difference between the intervention group and a comparison group (possibly from the previous year's cohort) in the percentage of students successfully completing all assignments, and whether this made a difference in students' grades. This almost certainly requires the school faculty to be using an online gradebook system with data that can be downloaded and analyzed at the school and classroom levels—a data environment that does exist in many schools with which we have worked, but may need to be adopted in others in order to engage in the kind of continuous improvement work we are advocating.

An Example Plan-Do-Study-Act Cycle of Inquiry for Providing Students with Opportunities to Set Mastery Goals and Improve Their Work

Plan. As a prelude to developing a specific intervention plan for mastery learning and opportunities to demonstrate growth in mastery, we recommend that the team of high school teachers interested in implementing this change idea discuss Myron Dueck's book *Grading Smarter, Not Harder.* The book is full of practical ideas about how to implement grading practices that help teachers to become more like coaches who are developing the skills of their students over time rather than judging those students based on their performance on a particular day and then moving on to the next skill. The ideas in this book (and associated tools on our website) can help the team to craft a specific plan of their own for the intervention.[33] The plan will almost certainly involve a set of course-related mastery goals, a system for students to monitor and track their progress over time, and opportunities for students to relearn content and/or skills and to demonstrate that learning through retesting and/or resubmitting assignments to demonstrate improved skills. And as noted in earlier examples, the team needs to identify the comparison group and plan for data collection.

Do. As the team implements the plan they have made, it is essential to collect the data that will help them to evaluate whether or not the change has led to improvements. This will involve such data collection as short pre- and postsurveys with students (using survey items like ones we include in the appendix). As described in the previous example, the data collection should also include intermediate measures of student outcomes (percent of assignments completed, growth in student mastery of course objectives over the quarter, report card grades, attendance, etc.). Data collection should also include teacher field notes (on at least a weekly basis) about how the change ideas seem to be working (barriers encountered, success stories observed, etc.).

Study. As we outlined earlier, at the end of the quarter the team needs to study the results of the intervention. Was there an increase in students' perception of the payoffs for exerting effort to learn course material and improve their skills when survey results from the beginning of the year are compared with end of the quarter results? (Is the average score higher, or is there a larger percentage of students selecting the high end of the scale range?) Was there an increase in completed assignments over that of the comparison group? Was there an improvement in student mastery levels and grades (and a decrease in failing quarter grades)? It is also important to discuss whether these results can be easily analyzed from online gradebook data. If not, what adaptations are needed to obtain data for analysis easily?

Act. Again, as we discussed above, the team would then make decisions based on the results of the Study phase about whether to continue the intervention as it is, to adapt it in some ways, or to move in another change direction if there appears to be little chance this approach will lead to improvement. There are certain to be lively discussions of whether the benefits of these practices justify the time costs involved.

Increasing Student Engagement Through Rigorous and Relevant Project-Based Learning

We have left this change idea until the end of our set of examples because it is perhaps the most ambitious and difficult one to implement. Even though there is evidence that project-based learning helps to increase student engagement, many barriers block the way for offering students this opportunity in schools and classrooms where it may be needed most.[34] Some districts specify curriculum and pacing guides in such a way that teachers see themselves as "going rogue" if they seek to make even small adaptations in assignments during particular units. Even if teachers have the freedom to use such an approach, the time it takes to plan for rigorous project-based learning units may be prohibitive. While project-based learning could potentially make a huge positive impact on student engagement and achievement outcomes, it can sometimes be too formidable to actually put into practice.

Because of this, it sometimes takes a small group of pioneers who are willing to take the lead and test out the idea on a small scale.

Such an effort is well-suited to a continuous improvement approach in which a team implements a change idea on a small scale while collecting and analyzing data around the effort to determine whether it led to any discernable improvements in student outcomes. This kind of intervention also fits well into a quarterly marking period.

What are we trying to accomplish? We remain focused on increasing the percentage of students who successfully earn their high school course credits. This inquiry examines whether a high interest and rigorous project-based learning unit can yield evidence in one's own school context of higher levels of student engagement (measured by attendance and self-reported student perceptions of engagement) and increased student success (measured by passing course grades).

What change might we introduce, and why? A team of at least two teachers from a core content area would agree to implement a project-based learning unit during one quarterly marking period and to conduct disciplined inquiry around its implementation and outcomes. As we noted earlier, our theory of action builds on research about students' desire to see the relevance of what they are learning, to experience choices and a sense of community in their schooling, and to engage in meaningful work. Research has shown some evidence of a positive effect of project-based learning on engagement and attitudes towards learning.[35]

An Example Plan-Do-Study-Act Cycle of Inquiry for a Project-Based Learning Intervention

Plan. We recommend that the team willing to try out this idea build on project-based learning (PBL) ideas created and tested by others. These are available from the Buck Institute of Education and many other sources.[36] Once the planning of the actual PBL unit is completed, the team would also need to designate treatment and comparison groups (as discussed earlier) and plan for data collection. As discussed earlier, it is helpful for the team conducting the PBL unit to keep systematic and regular notes about implementation issues. Self-report measures of student engagement, relevance of schoolwork, and meaningfulness of work (see survey items in the appendix) from before and after the unit would be useful metrics in addition to attendance and course grades, particularly if they can be collected electronically to reduce the work needed for data analysis. Although it can be more difficult to draw strong conclusions from qualitative data, it seems to us important to plan time for listening to student voices about their PBL experience, compared to other classroom experiences, to add to the data to be analyzed and consider in the Study and Act phases of the cycle. One might even consider adding several students to the continuous improvement team.

Do. The team then implements the PBL unit as planned and conducts the data collection around both implementation and student outcomes.

Study and Act. As the team analyzes results from the data collected, a major question is whether the time spent in implementing PBL actually yields significant enough benefits in student engagement and learning to be worth the while. There are certain to be hiccups in the early days of implementing PBL, and it may take time for these to be worked out sufficiently for benefits to be realized. It may well be necessary to change and adapt the details of the specific PBL unit and activities to obtain better results. The question often becomes one of how much time to invest. Student voices can be invaluable as the team considers this issue.

Implementing a Robotics Course to Increase Student Engagement in STEM Learning

Given the need to give ninth grade students engaging learning experiences that help to inspire them to exert effort in their academic courses, we believe that it is important to consider even bigger ideas, such as organizing the ninth grade schedule to include electives with opportunities for highly engaging active learning. We encourage schools who may have interested teachers to consider implementing a robotics elective for ninth graders. During our research experience conducting an independent quasi-experimental evaluation of a middle school summer robotics program, we found significant effects of the program on school attendance the following year.[37] We had the opportunity to observe middle school students deeply engaged in a robotics class, learning important skills as they worked in teams to build their robots, test them out, make adaptations, and prepare for the upcoming competition between teams. A robotics class can provide rich collaborative teamwork experiences and the opportunity to actively demonstrate learning as students make their robots perform. The experience offers a tight feedback loop in the learning experience as students observe ways to improve the performance of their robots and go back to make adaptations and try them out again. We observed students known to struggle academically become fully engaged in the learning experience in ways that could spur their learning and engagement in other areas. They saw the impact of their effort, built their self-efficacy, and took great pride in their work. Testing whether this intervention will also work with ninth graders makes a lot of sense. This evidence-based change idea will require substantial resources (including robotics equipment and teacher professional development), but it is likely to yield important benefits. We are hoping to hear of schools that take this idea and try it out using a cycle of inquiry process.

CONCLUDING THOUGHTS

What we have done in this chapter is to offer some practical examples of how school teams might engage in the continuous improvement disciplined inquiry process and how it could be applied with each of the overarching change idea umbrellas for improving high school outcomes we identified (early warning and intervention systems, family engagement, school connectedness, social-emotional learning, and instructional practices). Depending on the needs of the individual high school and the particular challenges schools face regarding ninth grade student success, other change ideas than those we highlighted may be more appropriate to implement first. For example, when large numbers of students are arriving at high school with insufficient reading and mathematics skills to tackle high school work, the district has a systemic issue of improving instruction and extra help strategies in the lower grades that requires focused attention. If chronic absence in ninth grade is strongly related to problems with attendance in the lower grades, the district must address those issues at earlier grade levels as well. The high school cannot make up for all the preceding problems that students bring with them without systematic district attention to those issues. At the same time, high school leaders can make progress in addressing the challenges that come with student needs. They may need to work with district leaders to identify evidence-based instructional programs that can be implemented during the transition summer or first semester to address reading and mathematics challenges faced by incoming students. Or their first priority might be implementing a more systematic tutoring program to help students during their first semester. If they are able to achieve consensual support from faculty, they may decide that creating an advisory period to increase personalized "nagging and nurturing" during the critical ninth grade year is the most promising path.[38] Schools must conduct their own needs assessments in order to decide on the particular evidence-based change ideas they think are best to implement first. In our work with the Cross State High School Redesign Collaborative (discussed in more detail in chapter 6) through the Everyone Graduates Center, we have seen the value of an intensive needs assessment process.[39]

The challenge of improving high school student outcomes is that multiple effective practices need to occur simultaneously for significant improvement to occur. As schools and districts continue to work through the iterative continuous improvement process, it is essential to keep "seeing the system" that is producing current outcomes and to consider how to make progress on multiple factors simultaneously. Learning from disciplined inquiry can occur within the school team engaged in continuous improvement activity, but learning that will lead to improved outcomes for more students will proceed more quickly if multiple teams are sharing their findings and learning from each other. It is to that improvement principle, "accelerating learning through networked communities," that we turn in chapter 6.[40]

CHAPTER 6

Building Networks to Share Learning About Improving High School Outcomes

Learning is a social process.[1] This is particularly the case for adults and professional learning. Much (if not all) of our learning occurs in interaction with other people. When we confront problems that we seek to solve in a continuous improvement framework, it makes sense to learn from the experience of others working on the same issues and to share what we are learning with them. The authors of *Learning to Improve* emphasize that learning is accelerated when we build networked learning communities to share our learning systematically.[2] We can begin to use the same measures and compare results of disciplined inquiry across different contexts. If we want to make progress at the speed it takes to actually make things better for students before they finish their schooling (and not just for those who may follow them long afterwards), we need to share our learning systematically.

Another benefit of working with others beyond one's own school is that it provides a means for the ideas and innovations developed by teachers, school leaders, and students in one school to have a longer life and greater impact. The people doing the work of educating and supporting students routinely come up with inventive, powerful, and spreadable solutions. But the majority of these solutions have very short lives. They exist in the classroom or school where they were invented often only as long as their inventor is in that classroom or school. When the inventor leaves, the change idea far too frequently evaporates from the school or district. Building connections between schools to routinely share findings, learnings, and solutions is an essential means to spread and sustain those powerful ideas.

In this chapter we share some of our experiences in building networked improvement communities over the past decade. The practitioners with whom we were working were not able to engage in the level of rigorous measurement and disciplined inquiry envisioned in *Learning to Improve*, but they made major strides as they shared their learning with each other and spurred each other on to try out change ideas and adapt in response to their learning. After we describe the learning process in these networked improvement communities, we offer some recommendations for how educational practitioners might begin to form such networked communities within their schools and districts or join those from other places. We conclude with some reflections about how to take these practitioner networks to the next level in accelerating their learning.

DIPLOMAS NOW PRINCIPALS NETWORK

One part of our work to transform practices in middle and high schools serving large numbers of students in poverty involved creating a network of principals focused on a common problem of practice. In the mid 2010s, a group of principals from our Diplomas Now schools decided to focus on the problem of high rates of student course failure, and how these rates were related to particular teacher grading practices.

This focus on grading and feedback practices grew out of a broader group discussion of the following diagnostic questions about instruction:

- Which students are missing what knowledge and skills assumed by grade level content?
- Are good lessons being consistently delivered and are students being asked to do quality coursework?
- How often do students end the day confused?
- Are students completing their class assignments?
- Are there effective second-chance opportunities for students to avoid failure?

The group also sought to explore the issue of what fuels student hope, given research on the relationship between student hope and academic outcomes.[3] After spending considerable time exploring these issues, the network decided to focus on reimagining grading and assessment from the students' perspective. The principal networked learning community experience included a several-hour meeting that allowed them to grow their own understanding of the issues, as well as other sessions for sharing their change ideas and how they were working. During their own learning sessions they discussed articles that addressed these grading issues (such as the issue of how averaging zeros on a 100-point grading scale has an inordinate negative impact on course grades, compared to averaging letter grades on a 0 to 4 point scale). The readings they discussed suggested alternative practices that maintained student motivation and provided opportunities for students to improve during the course.

Individual principals then decided on change ideas for their individual schools, implemented those changes, and had the opportunity to share back with the principals in the network about how their ideas were working. Principals implemented such ideas as transforming 100-point grading systems to more closely resemble the 0 to 4 point scale (in which failing grades do not pull down the average grade so dramatically), and transitioning to standards-based grading, with a focus on equipping teachers to analyze and adjust their instructional practices to help students better master the standards.[4] The network met all together twice a year for principals to share their experience with implementing ideas aimed at improving grading practices. Individual principals also engaged in conversations with colleagues and members of our team between those formal meetings.

As we reflected on the how the principals shared their learning with each other, we recognized the need for principals and their leadership teams to more systematically collect and analyze data about the impact of their change ideas on both teacher practices and student outcomes. Our principal network was only at the beginning stages of sharing their learning in ways that could lead to systematic improvement efforts and the scaling of significant improvement in student outcomes. It would also be important for multiple members within school-based teams to meet more frequently with teams from other schools.

CROSS STATE HIGH SCHOOL REDESIGN COLLABORATIVE

Since 2017 we have worked with a group of high schools from seven different states in a Cross State High School Redesign Collaborative (CSHSC). Together with partners from their states' Departments of Education, high schools in high-needs communities from Louisiana, Massachusetts, Mississippi, New Mexico, New York, Ohio, and Alabama, most of whom were identified under the Every Students Succeeds Act (ESSA) as needing comprehensive improvement, are seeking to work together within this collaborative to redesign themselves to become more effective in propelling adolescents to adult success in their communities in the twenty-first century.

Codeveloped by participating states, this design process leads schools through several stages. Schools begin by forming a diverse high school redesign team of eight to twelve members, including administrators, teachers, counselors, community members, and students. This team, which meets at least monthly and often more frequently, begins by conducting a comprehensive needs assessment and collecting student, teacher, and community input around design needs. As we argued with others in our *Great American High School Campaign* report, it is essential to "get the needs assessment right":

> For high schools and their communities to successfully position themselves for the 21st century, they need an accurate and shared understanding of the challenges they face and the foundations, both good and bad, from which they are starting. . . . States and districts need to use best practices in conducting their needs assessments and allow for customization based on a school's history, locale, student needs, capacity, and other factors that get at the type and intensity of reforms necessary.[5]

Next the high schools examine and customize evidence-based strategies on organizing adults, supporting students, teaching and learning, and creating equitable postsecondary pathways for all students, and adapted these to local circumstances. Within the CSHSC, this process involves regular meetings (three times a year) of the group of six to ten high school redesign teams within each state. The goal is to first create in-state networks and then, once trust and relationships are built among the participating schools in the state, link all the participating high schools across the seven states into a larger national network.

Besides receiving substantial guidance from state education agency leaders and the Everyone Graduates Center through a series of daylong workshops over the course of an initial design period, the school teams participating in this common redesign process share their learning with each other at meetings that occur three times a year. School teams across all seven states also have the opportunity to engage in virtual Problem of Practice sessions, in which the teams are invited to offer a presentation on a design challenge or innovation they wish to share with the network. Our Everyone Graduates Center team facilitates the network meeting of school teams in order to support deep understanding of the challenge and opportunities to gain from the wisdom of those attending. For example, one high school in New Mexico in their first year of redesign work shared the following design challenge: How do we develop a cohesive theme that connects all career pathways so that each pathway retains its individuality, while all students understand they are a part of the larger entity of the high school, regardless of their pathway?

Other networked community activities for school teams include conversation cafés and solution forums around specific topics or roles. Our center provides school teams with a protocol to prepare for "consultancies" during which they can share the latest iterations of their redesign plan with a partner school team, in preparation for feedback sessions with state and district leaders and members of the Everyone Graduates Center team.

NETWORKED LEARNING COMMUNITIES FOCUSED ON EARLY WARNING SYSTEMS

In our work with thirty-eight middle and high schools throughout New Mexico, we created a networked learning community of school teams that met monthly to share their learning with colleagues across the state. Even before COVID-19 hit, this had begun as a virtual networked learning community to facilitate participation from the many rural schools in the state (for whom travel to a common location could involve a day of travel each way). It follows a distance learning protocol initially developed by the University of New Mexico to meet rural health needs.[6] Each session begins with a brief expert presentation on a shared topic of interest. Then most of the community meetings involve presentations from school teams regarding their attempts to address particular problems of practice they encountered in setting up an early warning system to guide timely interventions with struggling students at their school, followed by all of the participating schools and experts in the session sharing their insights and ideas on how to address the challenge. Typical problems of practice included how to address such issues as student tardiness, student discipline problems, or classroom management issues, among others. In its early stages the learning community focused primarily on the development of promising change ideas rather than on analysis of how interventions had worked.

In another program, we are partnering with City Year in a Gates Foundation–funded Networks for School Improvement project focused on eighth grade on-track rates. The work started in middle schools in Milwaukee and is expanding into Tulsa and several additional districts. In its first year, teams at five middle schools, composed of teachers, counselors, administrators, and other support staff examined eighth grade early warning indicators in attendance, behavior, and course failure. Through a needs assessment and root cause analysis process the teams determined the highest leverage move was to start with a focus on student behavior. Over time this became an even more specific focus on student-teacher relationships. Teams from all five schools met several times a year to share their learning with respect to implementing change ideas related to improving student-teacher relationships at the grade, classroom, small group, and individual levels. The focus during the first year was on school teams learning the process of continuous improvement by focusing on relatively small change ideas that could be tested with one or more classrooms or a small group of students. The school teams worked to develop measurement strategies that would let them know their change ideas were working. This was a learning process, as initially teams would sometimes develop measurement strategies that were too elaborate to sustain or which did not directly measure the intervention. But by the end of the year, teams were able to present to each other a complete Plan-Do-Study-Act cycle, which included a data-informed assessment of whether they should adopt the change idea, work to modify and improve it, or abandon it. The goal for the second year was then to move to a large change idea, which could impact larger numbers of students. But just as progress was being made in this direction, COVID-19 hit. The work continued in virtual form, but needed to shift to change ideas that were COVID-19 relevant, with a focus on building a sense of belonging and engagement when schooling is remote.

NETWORKED LEARNING COMMUNITIES FOR SCHOOL FAMILY ENGAGEMENT TEAMS

Yet another recent initiative involved working with leaders in a western school district to equip members of family engagement action teams from the district's middle and high schools to more effectively engage and communicate with families as students make the transition to high school.[7] The ultimate goal was to improve ninth grade attendance and course passing outcomes through increased support and monitoring from families. The initiative provided professional development on ways to improve their family engagement efforts to teams from multiple schools. After a daylong workshop in the fall, in which teams from different schools were able to share their learning with each other, we organized at least two more meetings during the year for the teams to continue this process of sharing. Many of the same team members continued across the several years of the project as new school team members also joined. Team members were also linked together through email communications from a district facilitator, allowing them other opportunities to share their learning. Teams learned from each other about how to more effectively engage with immigrant families speaking languages other than English, ways to make high school information events for eighth grade families more effective, and strategies for using multiple means of communication. They also learned about communicating with families in a more timely way regarding student course grades and ways to help students turn around failing grades. Although we were not able to attain the level of rigorous and systematic study of change ideas we had hoped for, this networked learning community was a first step towards achieving the kind of accelerated learning advocated in *Learning to Improve*. We have also invited readers of our work on parent portal usage to share their learning with us in attempts to create a networked learning community focused on that specific problem of practice within family engagement for which common measures and systematic data analysis can be conducted.[8]

DISTRICT PRINCIPAL NETWORKS

To the extent that local districts have a group of several high schools with similar improvement needs, we believe that a district-led principal network is one of the best ways to build the kind of networked learning community that will advance and accelerate learning within districts. Leadership from within the district links the improvement work and principal accountability to district objectives in a way that leadership from external organizations cannot achieve. Ideally a skilled district leader with responsibility for high schools can lead principals (and potentially also their school-based teams) as they engage in systematic attempts at continuous improvement and share their learning with each other. Leadership that is both supportive and constructively challenging is essential for such a network to function effectively. We observed contrasting principal network meetings in one district: the group with the laissez-faire type district leader made much less progress in critical reflection about their work than did the group with a proactive district leader who demonstrated a well-balanced blend of supportive coaching and probing questions that provoked deeper reflection and analysis within the group. Extending this proactive district leadership to connect district principals (and their leadership teams) in common continuous improvement efforts and systematic sharing of their learning is an important next step. While this is occurring to some extent at the high school level, having more publicly available reports of how this is working and how district leaders can generate the kind of collaborative reflection that can spur and advance learning for school teams will contribute significantly to accelerating our learning about how to improve high school outcomes.[9]

RECOMMENDATIONS FOR DEVELOPING NETWORKED LEARNING COMMUNITIES

While the experiences we describe above can give you a flavor of what happens in a networked learning community and how it might be helpful, the goal is for those reading this book to engage in these kinds of networks themselves. How can you move in this direction?

Our primary recommendation is to begin at the school and district levels. If the improvement idea on which you are engaging in disciplined inquiry is an instructional change at the classroom level (like a couple of our examples in chapter 5), the networked community would begin with the (hopefully expanding) group of teachers engaged in trying out and studying a change idea—first at one school, and then at other schools within the district as the idea spreads. If the improvement idea is a school-level intervention (like the early warning system change ideas discussed in chapter 5), the network would ideally involve high school teams facilitated by a district office leader. Conducting network meetings monthly (or at least every other month) will facilitate shared learning at the school or district level.

As Bryk points out in *Improvement in Action,* expanding these networks requires creation of "improvement hubs" that facilitate communication among multiple teams, build the network's analytic capacity, and work to consolidate learning and spread improvement.[10] This requires considerable resources, and Bryk calls for substantial investment in a "national improvement infrastructure to accelerate educational improvements." We echo his call for resources to be invested in this way. But in the meantime, most educational practitioners and policy makers continue to face the challenge of limited resources for this work. How can we leverage the power of "less than optimal" networked communities in the context of limited resources?

Focusing on building a networked learning community at the district level can still yield substantial opportunities for accelerating learning until more extensive opportunities are available. The district in Menomonee Falls, Wisconsin is an example of a district that has internalized an improvement science orientation to its work with great success. Its work in fostering networked learning communities among its teachers and school leaders paid internal dividends that are now being shared with other district leaders.[11]

The Everyone Graduates Center at Johns Hopkins University is eager to hear of high school improvement efforts undertaken by educators influenced by what we have written, and to engage in follow-up discussions that can lead to further collaborations.[12] Given our own networks, we would probably also be able to connect you with others who are working on similar issues, including networks supported by the Carnegie Foundation or the Gates Foundation. Many states' education departments have staff devoted to this kind of continuous improvement work who could be helpful in connecting district teams together across the state.[13] More and more university schools of education have faculty and students trained in improvement science who may be willing to collaborate with schools and districts on continuous improvement initiatives, and connecting with these faculty to discuss collaborative initiatives can also be a first step towards building a network.

Even if we are not able in the short run to achieve the kind of networked improvement communities described by Bryk, we can begin on a smaller scale to move toward the kind of collaboration that can accelerate learning. The examples of networks we described in this chapter did advance the learning of those who participated in them in ways that trying to improve on their own could not achieve. We learned together with participants in these networks more about the issues related to trying to change grading practices, implement early warning systems, build greater school connectedness, and engage families more effectively during the transition to high school. Over time we have been able to equip school leaders to do more of the kind of data collection and analysis that can better inform the continuous improvement process. Taking the initiative to connect regularly with other school leaders to share experiences and learning around what is needed to improve high school outcomes is a critical first step.

CHAPTER 7

Confronting the Challenges and Seizing the Opportunities

We have sought in this practical guide to help equip readers to take the next steps in their journey of using improvement science to increase successful high school outcomes. The challenges are formidable. But standing still is not an option. And there may be unique opportunities to seize at this particular moment in our history. In this chapter we acknowledge and articulate some of the challenges that must be confronted. We suggest opportunities to leverage as you move forward in continuous improvement efforts focused on learning experiences and outcomes for high school students.

CHALLENGES IN THE WAKE OF COVID-19

As we write, schools continue to confront the challenges of the COVID-19 crisis. There is great concern that the gaps in student learning outcomes, fueled by the inequitable learning opportunities over the past year, have widened significantly.[1] There was wide variation in the amount of time it took schools and districts to shift to deliver virtual/online learning opportunities in the spring of 2020, in the readiness of teachers to shift to online instruction, and in the quality of that instruction across classrooms and schools. Significant numbers of students were not able to fully access online learning opportunities or to benefit from this mode of instructional delivery.

High schools, at least in some locales, have been particularly impacted by the health, education, and economic impacts of COVID-19. There are reports from across the nation on large increases in course failures and significant decreases in the percent of high school graduates immediately enrolling in college.[2] High school students have also forgone their own participation in schooling—either to help younger siblings learn remotely when their parents have to work outside of their home or to earn income to help support their family.[3] Thus, high schools will face challenges on how to enable students to rapidly recover learning and reengage them in schooling.

Besides the increased gaps in student learning and achievement that have resulted from COVID-related disruptions, there is sure to be a gap in resources available for schools and districts. Districts have already announced plans to address budget shortfalls caused by massive levels of unplanned expenditures necessitated by the COVID crisis. Staff layoffs are on the horizon if they have not already occurred. There may be short-term provisions from government sources to address the overwhelming educational needs, but there may well be a shortage of resources in years to come.

OPPORTUNITIES AFFORDED BY COVID-19

Although the coronavirus has brought extreme challenges on top of those already confronted, the crisis also opens the opportunity for significant redesign of educational systems in ways that improve students' educational experiences and outcomes. COVID-19 has created an environment open to new ideas on how to organize schools and conduct standard educational work processes. In the face of an unprecedented crisis, leaders are advocating a whole-system approach to continuous improvement.[4] At the school level, COVID-19 has also provided school leaders and teachers experience with many of the core processes of continuous improvement even though they were often not described as such. These include working collaboratively to design and test solutions for which no one has a clear answer, rapidly iterating in the face of constantly changing conditions, and seeking out insights from students, parents, and educators from other schools. Thus, more than ever before, both the need for and the possibility of employing a continuous improvement approach to improve student outcomes exist.

As a recent Brookings Institution report points out, the crisis has precipitated adaptations and innovations on a massive scale, which could potentially be harnessed in a continuous improvement effort to bring about transformation in standard educational work processes.[5] Many of these innovations involve the use of educational technology to support the instructional core. The Brookings Institution report suggests that innovative educational technologies that gained traction during COVID-19 can positively influence learning through:

> (1) scaling up quality instruction (by, for example, prerecorded lessons of high-quality teaching);
> (2) facilitating differentiated instruction (through, for example, computer-adaptive learning or live one-on-one tutoring);
> (3) expanding opportunities for student practice; and
> (4) increasing student engagement (through, for example, videos and games).[6]

As school teams consider how to improve high school student learning outcomes, it may be productive to study the impact of implementing more technology-based change ideas as supplemental instructional practices.

Schools have also become more proactive during the pandemic in scheduling individual and small group interactions with teachers in ways that could be contributing positively to learning. We believe that some of these innovations could be tested more systematically in classrooms as schools return to in-person learning. Creative educators can use the continuous improvement process we have outlined to test out change ideas to create opportunities for more personalized instruction and help build the student-teacher relationships that we know have a positive effect on student outcomes. Almost more than anything, COVID-19 has shown parents and teachers that learning is a social-emotional process and success in school requires an integrated approach to social, emotional, and academic development. How to do this in practice, however, is not fully known, and as such is a question tailor-made for continuous improvement approaches.

COVID-19 forced schools and districts to become more flexible in their responses to students' educational needs. Having learned to be more flexible, they need to continue this orientation of willingness to adapt their practices more readily to student needs. This may take the form of such innovations as more flexible scheduling, alternatives to seat-time requirements, greater opportunities to replace requirements with online community college courses, and other alternative pathways.[7] Figuring out how to make these more global innovations work in a particular school is where schools will need to embrace continuous improvement.

The Brookings Report also points out that the COVID-19 crisis has forced schools to make family engagement a much higher priority than it had been previously, particularly at the higher grade levels. School staff have had to work more closely with families than ever before. It is likely that schools have the ability to text more families than ever before, and that the barriers we observed in many schools (like missing phone numbers or consent for receiving text messaging) have been lessened. The family engagement adaptations and innovations born of COVID-19 can be leveraged for the future as schools have gained more experience in proactively working with students' families.

The coronavirus crisis also appears to have encouraged schools and districts to listen more than ever before to the experiences of and suggestions from students and families, the frontline education stakeholders.[8] This is one of the most crucial principles of continuous improvement: listening to the voices of those most closely affected. As our colleague Richard Lofton has emphasized in his "Nobody Asked Me" campaign, we need to address our failure to talk with those most closely affected by the school experience—the students themselves.[9] This is particularly the case for historically underserved students and their families. Schools and districts will do well to continue this work of listening more frequently and closely to students and their families once the pandemic period has passed.

CONFRONTING THE CHALLENGES TO WIDESPREAD USE OF CONTINUOUS IMPROVEMENT IN SCHOOLS

Continuous improvement approaches have considerable potential for helping schools address the impact of COVID-19. But we must find ways to address the barriers standing in the way of widespread adoption of improvement science and continuous improvement activities in school districts and high schools. Those barriers include real and perceived lack of time, measurement and data challenges, and system actors with a vested interest in the status quo.

Real and Perceived Lack of Time

The continuous improvement process takes time—a resource in short supply at most schools. Besides the time for meetings to plan and reflect and study, the process requires time for data collection and analysis. Data may need to be input manually if technological solutions are not readily available. Implementing interventions takes time—and the individuals who do this work need to be paid for their time. And as we noted in chapter 3, schools actually need multiple improvement teams working on multiple issues simultaneously. Finding this time is a real challenge. Districts may want to consider some of the lessons learned from COVID-19 about creative reorganization of schedules and flexible use of time as they move forward. One of the perhaps unintended consequences of COVID-19 was that in some circumstances teachers spent fewer total hours per week in front of classrooms delivering instruction. In some cases, this provided more time for collaborative work and professional learning. The United States has always been among the nations in which teachers spend more time on their own teaching and less time working with their colleagues to improve their craft and generate school improvements. As schools and districts return to "normal," this moment in history calls for reflection about how we can dismantle some of the systematic barriers to providing teachers with the time to work collaboratively to improve student and school outcomes. How can we use time differently for both teachers and students? Schools and districts may also want to consider how they can use instructional time to engage students in real-world problem solving—beginning with the problems of their own high schools. Engaging students themselves in the continuous improvement process as part of their regular instruction time could be revolutionary.

Besides the challenge of real shortages of time, schools face a perceived shortage of time to engage in a rigorous improvement process. For two decades schools have felt pressure to get better now—or at the very least by the end of the year. This creates an environment where false steps or ideas that do not pan out are feared. Yet learning and adapting from ideas that did not work is central to continuous improvement, and one of the engines which drives its impact. School improvement that results in better student outcomes is hard. It seldom goes in a linear fashion. We need to hold onto some of the humility COVID-19 brought, and create accountability structures that will not penalize schools when their efforts to try evidence-based ideas within a continuous learning process do not immediately pan out.

Measurement and Data Challenges

Second, school and district teams may struggle with the measurement and data components of the improvement process. In our experience, school teams may often select data collection methods that are not practical or sustainable. Even though multiple observations in multiple classrooms each week may be the best way to understand how a change idea is working, it is probably impossible to carry out. Or teams may even experience difficulty with identifying appropriate measures that can be collected and analyzed to determine whether change is actually leading to improvement. There may also be technical challenges associated with accessing and arranging data in ways that can advance the cycles of inquiry in the improvement process. School personnel may be unfamiliar with how to get the district data system to run appropriate reports, or how to manipulate the data in a spreadsheet once it is downloaded. We have also encountered FERPA-related concerns for data privacy issues that can hinder the process of sharing student information (including details about interventions) across members of the school team. Districts will need to devote resources to supporting schools in accessing data in usable form and developing systems that allow ways to share data in secure ways in the interest of promoting student success. Providing stipends for teacher leaders with particular talents in data management and analysis could be a cost-effective strategy. Investing in continuous improvement training for district research staff so that they can support schools around measurement and data collection in the cycle of inquiry process will also yield important benefits.

Elements of the System with Vested Interests in the Status Quo

At a broader level, challenges arise when change ideas or findings from cycles of inquiry confront dimensions of the educational system (such as particular central office departments) with vested interests in the status quo and sometimes adamant resistance to proposed changes. Districts may have invested in particular curricula or data management systems, and district leaders may not want to consider evidence that suggests the need for change. Teachers may oppose changes in contracts that require additional time commitments or redistribution of responsibilities. Changing school schedules may disrupt the entire district transportation system. Districts that make a serious commitment to continuous improvement will need to create crosscutting organizational structures that can facilitate hard conversations about the potentially disruptive findings of the systems analysis undertaken by improvement teams. They will need to be willing to challenge the status quo.

FINDING THE ACTIVATION ENERGY TO MOVE SYSTEMS TO HIGHER PERFORMANCE

Leveraging these opportunities will require a concerted commitment to seeing the system within which our education problems are situated and understanding what it takes to address multiple system issues simultaneously. In many ways, educational systems are like thermodynamic systems that may require a high level of kinetic activation energy to move them to higher performance. Just as it takes much more energy to roll a ball uphill than to get it moving downhill (where gravity can contribute to its progress), so it is with improving educational systems. This is particularly the case within systems affected dramatically by concentrated poverty and its associated effects on student health, experience of trauma, and learning opportunities. Schools and districts may have the will to engage in the continuous improvement process we have articulated here, but where will they find the resources to sustain their attempts to launch such a process? Continuous improvement work requires energy—a commodity that is in short supply in schools that operate under conditions of stress and scarcity.

Anthony Bryk has called for a "standing national infrastructure" of improvement organizations focused on diverse educational problems that could serve to support schools and districts.[10] We echo Bryk's call for such an investment. There are many deeply entrenched problems to solve in thousands of districts and tens of thousands of schools across the United States, and millions more across the globe. These complex problems require the concentrated attention of teams of individuals with a deep understanding of educational systems, of the factors that make for effective instruction, and of how to lead adults to change their practices. School and district leaders need the help of organizations with deep wells of experience in helping educators in the continuous improvement process.

In the meantime (or if such resources remain out of reach), we also propose that schools and districts leverage nearby, lower-cost resources that they may not yet have considered. When districts are located near universities with graduate education programs, their leaders would do well to explore the willingness of research faculty and their students to offer voluntary collaboration as part of their graduate programs. The Institute for Education Sciences has encouraged such practical training of predoctoral students in working together with education practitioners on initiatives to improve student outcomes, and even universities that do not have sponsored funding for such training are moving in this direction in their programs. Those with experience formulating research questions and working with data could make invaluable contributions to schools and districts pursuing continuous improvement in several ways. Even without formal coaching roles they would add value to brainstorming sessions as well as in operationalizing, collecting, and analyzing data. Graduate students (and faculty) will gain deep understanding of the educational issues they are studying while they provide some of the needed "boots on the ground" to accomplish the work of continuous improvement. These university partners may not have the breadth of continuous improvement experience that the organizations Bryk envisions possess, but they may well have sufficient training and experience in continuous improvement to help advance the work in schools and districts located nearby.

Pairing Continuous Improvement with Structural and Comprehensive Reforms in the Highest Need Schools

One of the challenges the continuous improvement framework will need to address is how to combine efforts to improve multiple dimensions of instruction and school organization simultaneously, both within individual schools and across all schools within districts. In the nation's schools that face the greatest concentration of student needs and serve historically underserved communities, the activation energy required for positive change will necessitate pairing a continuous improvement framework with structural and comprehensive supports. This is the case even if schools can manage to mobilize several different teams working on different dimensions of the problem simultaneously. One of the key learnings from our Diplomas Now project is that when a high school has hundreds of students with off-track indicators (chronic absenteeism, behavioral challenges, or course failures), almost all available adult time and energy is spent, often unsuccessfully, meeting immediate student needs. Until the pressure of addressing immediate student needs is relieved through structural changes that help address these needs, school leaders and teachers will not have the time or energy to work collectively to improve outcomes. Efforts that combine comprehensive school reform with an early warning and tiered intervention system and additional student supports are needed. Fortunately, there are growing examples of the types of structural and comprehensive responses that can help, such as Diplomas Now, the Network for College Success, New Visions, Connecticut Rise, CORE districts, and the BARR model.[11] These models involve progress monitoring of all students on predictive indicators with multitiered systems of support, and may bring in additional person-power through AmeriCorps programs like City Year to enable all students to have supportive relationships, mentoring, and tutoring. All of these efforts have also created networks which provide the means for schools to improve together and learn from each other. Comprehensive reforms may include such structural components as ninth grade academies built around interdisciplinary teacher teams that share common and manageable numbers of students. They may also include the formation of Community Schools that identify out-of-school challenges to success in school and then assemble community and social sector assets to address those needs. To realize the power of continuous improvement in our schools that serve high concentrations of students who live in poverty, we will need to make it a part of a larger improvement effort.

CONCLUDING THOUGHTS

As we reflect back on our participation in the past twenty-five years of school reform, we view the continuous improvement framework as an important corrective to the zigzag pattern produced by a reform pendulum that has swung widely between centralization and decentralization, sanctions and incentives, inputs and outputs.[12] Our own work over nearly three decades has been closely connected to the progression from more school-centric comprehensive school reform to efforts more focused on systemic district-level reform efforts. We observed at close hand the movement toward privatization as large districts with which we were working contracted with external school operators and built portfolio systems of schools, closing many of them along the way. We experienced school turnaround efforts relying on human capital infusion that sometimes yielded positive results but more frequently did not. And we observed the negative effects on children who returned to buildings where nearly all the adults had turned over and there were no familiar faces or relationships. Our work within a continuous improvement framework over the past several years has reconfirmed for us the importance of close attention to the working of systems at all levels—from classrooms (and subsystems within classrooms) to the district system and how it is influenced by factors outside it (neighborhood and local, state, and federal contexts). Simplistic appeals to accountability structures or finding "better human capital" or increasing school leader autonomy have not worked sufficiently. Attempts at comprehensive school reform—addressing instruction, school organization, climate, family engagement, and other components simultaneously—have yielded varying degrees of positive results, depending on the context. The continuous improvement approach has helped to focus many more eyes upon the "system" and the importance of addressing individual problems in light of the system contributing to those problems. It also enables networks of schools which face common challenges to learn collectively, share insights, and rapidly spread effective approaches, combating the isolation many schools and school leaders feel when they are asked to reform alone. And yet, as we have argued above, the size of the problem in many of our nation's high schools requires a comprehensive approach that tackles multiple dimensions (school climate and organization, instruction, professional development, data monitoring and intervention systems) simultaneously. We must use the continuous improvement framework within a more comprehensive approach to making high schools work for all the students they serve. It is then essential for us to work together to share our learning through networked communities if we are to solve the problems of our nation's high schools. We invite you to join us in this endeavor.[13]

APPENDIX

Student Survey (Perception) Measures

As noted in chapter 4, student perception measures are often useful in the continuous improvement process. To keep the process simple, it is most helpful to collect these through very short surveys (taking five minutes or less) administered to students electronically if possible. Different measures will be appropriate for different interventions and inquiry cycles. This appendix provides a bank of potential measures and information about where they may be accessed. The continuous improvement process may lead to creating even better measures, but we offer these as a way to get started.

Student survey measures for the following classroom climate constructs (three items per construct) are available on the Project for Education Research That Scales (PERTS) website:[1]

Affirming cultural identity

- Classroom belonging
- Feedback for growth

- Meaningful work
- Student voice
- Teacher caring

The following items were used in Everyone Graduates Center student surveys in several different projects over the past decades. Students are asked to select a response from a 4-point scale (agree strongly, agree somewhat, disagree somewhat, disagree strongly). The wording can be adapted for particular classes.

Student perception of school connectedness

- Most days I enjoy coming to school.
- I feel safe at this school.
- I don't really care about school (reverse coded).

Student behavioral engagement (4-point scale: never, sometimes, very often, all the time)

- I pay attention in my classes.
- I stay on task in my classes.
- I complete all my schoolwork.

Student interest-related engagement

- I like what I am learning in my classes.
- I think what we are learning in my classes is interesting.
- I've given up on being interested in school (reverse coded).

Student perception of relevance of schoolwork

- My classes prepare me for what I plan to do in life.
- What I learn in my classes is important for my future.
- Working hard in my classes will matter for my future success in a career.

STUDENT PERCEPTION OF PARENTAL SCHOOL SUPPORT

The following items are from a survey by Sharon Paulsen.[2] Students are asked to select a response from a 4-point scale (agree strongly, agree somewhat, disagree somewhat, disagree strongly).

Values toward achievement items

- My parent/guardian tries to get me to do my best on everything I do.
- My parent/guardian has high aspirations for my future.
- My parent/guardian thinks that getting ahead in life is very important.

Interest in schoolwork items

- My parent/guardian makes sure that I have done my homework.
- My parent/guardian usually knows the grades I get.
- My parent/guardian seldom looks at my tests and papers from school (reverse coded).

Involvement in school functions items

- My parent/guardian usually goes to parent-teacher conferences.
- My parent/guardian usually goes to activities in which I am involved in school.
- My parent/guardian sometimes does volunteer work at my school.

STUDENT PERCEPTION OF AUTONOMY IN THE CLASSROOM

The PERTS survey includes three items on "student voice" that provide a measure of students' perception of autonomy or choice. The following items are a survey conducted by Erik Ruzek and colleagues.[3] Those authors used a 5-point scale (from not at all true to very true), but a 4-point scale (disagree strongly to agree strongly) would also work. The last item (about lively discussions) could be eliminated if the goal is to strictly measure autonomy.

- Students often get to make decisions about how the class is run.
- Students often get choices about how to do projects or assignments.
- Students often feel like they get to help lead the class.
- The teacher changes what's planned to make it more interesting for students.
- We have a lot of lively discussions.

These student autonomy items are from a survey conducted by Corliss Bean and colleagues.[4] They can be used with either the 5-point or 4-point scales described above.

- I felt that my teacher provided us with choices and options.
- The teacher listened to how we would like to do things.
- The teacher helped us to really understand the goals of the class and what we need to do.
- The teacher tried to understand how we see things before suggesting new ways to do things.

STUDENT PERCEPTIONS OF GRADING PRACTICES

We offer the following suggestions for student survey items related to grading practices (using either the 4- or 5-point scales described above):

- The grading system in this class helps motivate me to work hard.
- The grading system in this class helps me want to improve my writing.
- If I didn't learn something in time for the test in this class, I have another chance to show what I have learned.
- The grading system in this class is fair.
- If I work hard, I feel I can succeed in this class.

Notes

Introduction

1. Gary Orfield, ed., *Dropouts in America: Confronting the Graduation Rate Crisis* (Cambridge, MA: Harvard Education Press, 2004).
2. Bob Wise, *Raising the Grade: How High School Reform Can Save Our Youth and Our Nation* (San Francisco: Jossey-Bass, 2008).
3. Daniel Princiotta, "Understanding the Great U.S. High School Graduation Rate Rise: 1998-2010" (PhD diss., Johns Hopkins University, 2019).
4. Matthew Atwell et al., *Building a Grad Nation: Progress and Challenge in Raising High Graduation Rates* (Washington, DC, and Baltimore: Civic Enterprises and Everyone Graduates Center, Johns Hopkins University, 2019), https://www.americaspromise.org/2019-building-grad-nation-report.
5. Princiotta, "Understanding the Great U.S. High School Graduation Rate Rise."
6. Atwell et al., *Building a Grad Nation.*
7. Megan Kuhfeld et al., "Projecting the Potential Impacts of COVID-19 School Closures on Academic Achievement," *Educational Researcher* 49, no. 8 (November 2020): 549–65, doi:10.3102/0013189X20965918.
8. Valerie Strauss, "More Students Than Ever Got F's in First Term of 2020-21 School Year—But Are A-F Grades Fair in a Pandemic?," *Washington Post*, December 6, 2020, https://www.washingtonpost.com/education/2020/12/06/more-students-than-ever-got-fs-first-term-2020-21-school-year-are-a-f-grades-fair-pandemic/. The article cites data from five different states.
9. Anthony S. Bryk et al., *Learning to Improve: How America's Schools Can Get Better at Getting Better* (Cambridge, MA: Harvard Education Press, 2015).
10. Consortium on Chicago School Research, *Freshman Year: The Make-it or Break-it Year* (Chicago: Consortium on Chicago School Research, 2007), https://files.eric.ed.gov/fulltext/ED498354.pdf; Emily Krone Phillips, *The Make-or-Break Year: Solving the Dropout Crisis One Ninth Grader at a Time* (New York: The New Press, 2019); Elaine Allensworth and John Q. Easton, *What Matters for Staying On-Track and Graduating in Chicago Public Schools: A Close Look at Course Grades, Failures, and Attendance in the Freshman Year* (Chicago: Consortium on Chicago School Research, 2007),

https://consortium.uchicago.edu/publications/what-matters-staying-track-and-graduating-chicago-public-schools; and Martha Abele Mac Iver and Matthew Messel, "The ABCs of Keeping On Track to Graduation: Research Findings from Baltimore," *Journal of Education for Students Placed at Risk (JESPAR)* 18, no. 1 (2013): 50–67, doi:10.1080/10824669.2013.745207.

11. Shane J. Lopez, *Gallup Student Poll National Report* (Washington, DC: Gallup Student Poll and America's Promise Alliance, 2009), https://www.americaspromise.org/sites/default/files/d8/legacy/bodyfiles/GSP%20National%20Report.pdf.
12. John Q. Easton, Esperanza Johnson, and Lauren Sartain, *The Predictive Power of Ninth-Grade GPA* (Chicago: UChicago Consortium on School Research, 2017), https://consortium.uchicago.edu/publications/predictive-power-ninth-grade-gpa; and Martha Abele Mac Iver and Matthew Messel, *Predicting High School Outcomes in the Baltimore City Public Schools,* The Senior Urban Education Research Fellowship Series, vol. 7 (Washington, DC: Council of the Great City Schools, 2012), https://files.eric.ed.gov/fulltext/ED536739.pdf.
13. Students can certainly recover and attend college, but in our experience the failing grade may mean that certain colleges will not offer them admission.
14. Michelle Fine, *Framing Dropouts: Notes on the Politics of an Urban Public High School* (Albany, NY: SUNY Press, 1991), 77.
15. See, for example, the Seattle Public Schools Strategic Plan, in which one of the primary goals is to "Increase on-time graduation by making sure each student has at least six credits by the end of 9th grade." "Strategic Plan Update," Seattle Public Schools, https://www.seattleschools.org/district/calendars/news/what_s_new/strategic_plan_update_superintendent_denise_juneau.
16. Lora Cohen-Vogel et al., "Implementing Educational Innovations at Scale: Transforming Researchers into Continuous Improvement Scientists," *Educational Policy* 29, no. 1 (January 2015): 257–77, doi:10.1177/0895904814560886; Marisa Cannata, Lora Cohen-Vogel, and Michael Sorum, "Partnering for Improvement: Improvement Communities and Their Role in Scale Up," *Peabody Journal of Education* 92, no. 5 (2017): 569–88, doi:10.1080/0161956X.2017.1368633; Sandra Park et al., *Continuous Improvement in Education* (Stanford, CA: Carnegie Foundation for the Advancement of Teaching, 2013), https://www.carnegiefoundation.org/wp-content/uploads/2014/09/carnegie-foundation_continuous-improvement_2013.05.pdf; Heather Hough, Erika Byun, and Laura Mulfinger, *Using Data for Improvement: Learning from the CORE Data Collaborative* (Stanford, CA: Policy Analysis for California Education, September 2018), https://gettingdowntofacts.com/sites/default/files/GDTFII_Report_Hough.pdf; Heather Hough et al., *Continuous Improvement in Practice* (Stanford, CA: Policy Analysis for California Education, November 2017), https://www.edpolicyinca.org/sites/default/files/CI%20in%20Pratice.pdf; and Karen Shakman et al., *Continuous Improvement in Education: A Toolkit for Schools and Districts*, REL 2021–014 (Washington, DC: US Department of Education, Institute of Education Sciences, National Center for Education Evaluation and Regional Assistance, Regional Educational Laboratory Northeast & Islands, 2020), https://ies.ed.gov/ncee/edlabs/regions/northeast/pdf/REL_2021014.pdf.
17. Bryk et al., *Learning to Improve.*

18. Bryk et al., *Learning to Improve*, 57.
19. Nettie Legters et al., *Comprehensive Reform for Urban High Schools: A Talent Development Approach* (New York: Teachers College Press, 2002).
20. Robert Balfanz and Nettie Legters, *Locating the Dropout Crisis* (Baltimore: Center for Research on the Education of Students Placed At Risk, Johns Hopkins University, 2004), https://eric.ed.gov/?id=ED484525.
21. Robert Balfanz, Liza Herzog, and Douglas J. Mac Iver. "Preventing Student Disengagement and Keeping Students on the Graduation Path in Urban Middle-Grades Schools: Early Identification and Effective Interventions," *Educational Psychologist* 42, no. 4 (2007): 223–35, doi:10.1080/00461520701621079.
22. William Corrin et al., Addressing Early Warning Indicators: Interim Impact Findings from the Investing in Innovation (i3) Evaluation of Diplomas Now (New York: MDRC, 2016), https://www.mdrc.org/publication/addressing-early-warning-indicators.
23. For a description of EGC's work, see www.every1graduates.org.
24. Robert Balfanz, "The Path from Velvet Rope Lines to Diplomas Now and More," https://education.jhu.edu/csos/about/celebrating-50-years/.
25. Martha Abele Mac Iver, Robert Balfanz, and Vaughan Byrnes, *Advancing the "Colorado Graduates" Agenda: Understanding the Dropout Problem and Mobilizing to Meet the Graduation Challenge* (Denver: Colorado Children's Campaign, 2009), https://files.eric.ed.gov/fulltext/ED539116.pdf; Joanna Fox and Vaughn Byrnes, *Getting Back On-Track: Early Warning Indicator Analysis of High School & Post-Secondary Outcomes, San Jose Unified School District* (Baltimore: Johns Hopkins University Everyone Graduates Center, 2015), https://new.every1graduates.org/getting-back-on-track-san-jose/; Mac Iver and Messel, "The ABCs of Keeping On Track to Graduation."
26. Bryk et al., *Learning to Improve*.

Chapter 1

1. Anthony S. Bryk et al., *Learning to Improve: How America's Schools Can Get Better at Getting Better* (Cambridge, MA: Harvard Education Press, 2015), 24.
2. We prefer the term *stakeholder* over the term *user* (from *Learning to Improve*) to refer to the groups involved in and served by schools and the educational system.
3. Sarah McKay, "Problem-Centered Policy Making," Carnegie Commons Blog, February 18, 2015, https://www.carnegiefoundation.org/blog/problem-centered-policy-making/.
4. Daniel Princiotta and Ryan Reyna, *Achieving Graduation for All: A Governor's Guide to Dropout Prevention and Recovery* (Washington, DC: National Governors Association Center for Best Practices, 2009), https://files.eric.ed.gov/fulltext/ED507071.pdf.
5. Elaine Allensworth, "The Use of Ninth-Grade Early Warning Indicators to Improve Chicago Schools," *Journal of Education for Students Placed at Risk (JESPAR)* 18, no. 1 (2013): 68–83, doi:10.1080/10824669.2013.7451. While performance in ninth grade remains the most important predictor of high school success, recent research findings also encourage district and school leaders to pay more attention to "the forgotten year" of tenth grade as well.

See Alex Seeskin, Shelby Mahaffie, and Alexandra Usher, *The Forgotten Year: Applying Lessons from Freshman Success to Sophomore Year* (Chicago: UChicago Consortium on School Research, 2020), https://consortium.uchicago.edu/publications/the-forgotten-year.

6. Although what we propose in this paragraph seems intuitively obvious, we have been surprised in some of our work with districts not to find such teams already in place.
7. Martha Abele Mac Iver, "When Minimum Grading Policies Backfire: Who Decides Whether to Let Students Fail?," in *When School Policies Backfire: How Well-Intended Measures Can Harm Our Most Vulnerable Students*, ed. Michael A. Gottfried and Gilberto Q. Conchas (Cambridge, MA: Harvard Education Press, 2016), 69–84.
8. Paul Tough, "What If the Secret to Success Is Failure?" *New York Times Magazine*, September 14, 2011.
9. Mac Iver, "When Minimum Grading Policies Backfire."
10. Camille Farrington, *Failing at School: Lessons for Redesigning Urban High Schools* (New York: Teachers College Press, 2014).
11. "First Amendment—Retaliation: District Court Denies School District's Request for Summary Judgment After Administrator Directed Staff Not to Follow Board-Approved Grading Scale," Ohio School Boards Association website, http://www.ohioschoolboards.org/school-law-summary-2012-3-and-2012-4-5#SLS12-3o; also see Goudeau v. East Baton Rouge Parish School Bd., 951 F.Supp.2d 874 (M.D. La. 2012), http://www.leagle.com/decision/In%20Adv%20FDCO%20140313-000106.
12. Stephen R. Covey, *The 7 Habits of Highly Effective People: An Extraordinary Step-by-Step Guide to Achieving the Human Characteristics That Really Create Success* (New York: Simon and Schuster, 1989); also see Martha Abele Mac Iver, "Beginning with the End in Mind: The District Office Leadership Role in Closing the Graduation Gap for At-Risk Students," *Educational Considerations* 38, no. 1 (2010): 8–16, doi:10.4148/0146-9282.1121.
13. David M. Quinn, "Experimental Evidence on Teachers' Racial Bias in Student Evaluation: The Role of Grading Scales," *Educational Evaluation and Policy Analysis* 42, no. 3 (September 2020): 375–92, doi:10.3102/0162373720932188; Harriet R. Tenenbaum and Martin D. Ruck, "Are Teachers' Expectations Different for Racial Minority Than for European American Students? A Meta-Analysis," *Journal of Educational Psychology* 99, no. 2 (2007): 253–73, doi:10.1037/0022-0663.99.2.253; and John M. Malouff and Einar B. Thorsteinsson, "Bias in Grading: A Meta-Analysis of Experimental Research Findings," *Australian Journal of Education* 60, no. 3 (November 2016): 245–56, doi:10.1177/0004944116664618.
14. See https://www.nobodyaskedmebmore.org/.
15. Quotation from interview participant in Richard Lofton, "Understanding Black Urbanism Through the Complexities of the Black Habitus" (lecture, Center for Urban Research and Learning, Loyola University Chicago, November 20, 2020).
16. From the video "It Really, Actually Changed My Life" posted on the PBLWorks website, https://my.pblworks.org/resource/video/it_really_actually_changed_my_life.

17. "It Really, Actually Changed My Life."

Chapter 2

1. Anthony S. Bryk et al., *Learning to Improve: How America's Schools Can Get Better at Getting Better* (Cambridge, MA: Harvard Education Press, 2015), 46.
2. H. Dickson Corbett and B. L. Wilson, "The Central Office Role in Instructional Improvement," *School Effectiveness and School Improvement* 3, no. 1 (1992): 45–68, doi:10.1080/0924345920030105.
3. Corbett and Wilson, "The Central Office Role," 46.
4. Bryk, *Learning to Improve*, 21.
5. See Elaine Allensworth and John Q. Easton, *What Matters for Staying On-Track and Graduating in Chicago Public Schools: A Close Look at Course Grades, Failures, and Attendance in the Freshman Year* (Chicago: Consortium on Chicago School Research, 2007), https://consortium.uchicago.edu/publications/what-matters-staying-track-and-graduating-chicago-public-schools; Elaine Allensworth, "The Use of Ninth-Grade Early Warning Indicators to Improve Chicago Schools," *Journal of Education for Students Placed at Risk (JESPAR)* 18, no. 1 (2013): 68–83, doi:10.1080/10824669.2013.745181; Martha Abele Mac Iver and Matthew Messel, *Predicting High School Outcomes in the Baltimore City Public Schools*, The Senior Urban Education Research Fellowship Series, vol. 7 (Washington, DC: Council of the Great City Schools, 2012), https://files.eric.ed.gov/fulltext/ED536739.pdf; Ruth Curran Neild and Robert Balfanz, *Unfulfilled Promise: The Dimensions and Characteristics of Philadelphia's Dropout Crisis, 2000–2005* (Philadelphia: Philadelphia Youth Transitions Collaborative, 2006), https://files.eric.ed.gov/fulltext/ED538341.pdf; Ruth Curran Neild, Scott Stoner-Eby, and Frank Furstenberg, "Connecting Entrance and Departure: The Transition to Ninth Grade and High School Dropout," *Education and Urban Society* 40, no. 5 (July 2008): 543–69, doi:10.1177/0013124508316438; and David Silver, Marisa Saunders, and Estela Zarate, *What Factors Predict High School Graduation in the Los Angeles Unified School District: California Dropout Research Project Report #14* (Santa Barbara, CA: California Dropout Research Project, 2008), http://cdrpsb.org/dropouts/researchreport14.pdf.
6. Elaine Allensworth and Kallie Clark, "High School GPAs and ACT Scores as Predictors of College Completion: Examining Assumptions About Consistency Across High Schools," *Educational Researcher* 49, no. 3 (April 2020): 198–211, doi:10.3102/0013189X20902110.
7. Research in New York City found that middle school retention, but not elementary school retention, was associated with a higher probability of failure to graduate. See Louis T. Mariano, Paco Martorell, and Tiffany Berglund, *How Does Repeating a Grade Impact Students' High School Persistence and Behavior? The Case of New York City* (Santa Monica, CA: RAND Corporation, 2018), https://www.rand.org/pubs/research_briefs/RB10025.html. Research in Baltimore, on the other hand, found that being over-age for grade in sixth grade (an indicator of prior retention in grade) was a significant predictor of nongraduation. See Baltimore Education Research Consortium, *Destination Graduation: Sixth Grade Early Warning Indicators for Baltimore City*

Schools (Baltimore: Baltimore Education Research Consortium, 2011), http://baltimore-berc.org/pdfs/SixthGradeEWIFullReport.pdf.

8. See Kevin Mabie, "A Mixed-Methods Comparison of Standards-Based and Traditional Gradebooks in One High School" (EdD diss., Lindenwood University, 2014), https://eric.ed.gov/?id=ED567452.
9. Martha Abele Mac Iver et al., "Urban Parents at the Portal: Family Use of Web-Based Information on Student Course Grades," *School Community Journal* (forthcoming 2021). For evidence of the positive effects of parent portal usage from randomized control trials, see Peter Bergman, *Technology Adoption in Education: Usage, Spillovers and Student Achievement*, CESifo Working Paper No. 6101 (Munich: Ludwig Maximilians University Center for Economic Studies & Ifo Institute, 2016), https://www.cesifo.org/en/publikationen/2016/working-paper/technology-adoption-education-usage-spillovers-and-student; and Peter Bergman, "Nudging Technology Use: Descriptive and Experimental Evidence from School Information Systems," *Education Finance and Policy* 15, no. 4 (2020): 623–47, doi:10.1162/edfp_a_00291.
10. Bryk et al., *Learning to Improve*, 46.
11. Bryk et al., *Learning to Improve*, 57.

Chapter 3

1. Anthony S. Bryk et al., *Learning to Improve: How America's Schools Can Get Better at Getting Better* (Cambridge, MA: Harvard Education Press, 2015), 57.
2. Jessica Levin and Meredith Quinn, *Missed Opportunities: How We Keep High-Quality Teachers Out of Urban Classrooms* (New York: The New Teacher Project, 2003), https://tntp.org/assets/documents/MissedOpportunities.pdf.
3. Martha Abele Mac Iver, "Little Things Count: Principal and New Teacher Feedback About District Support in the Hiring Process," *ERS Spectrum* 24, no. 2 (2006): 41.
4. "5 Whys: Getting to the Root of a Problem Quickly," Mind Tools, https://www.mindtools.com/pages/article/newTMC_5W.htm; Patty Mulder, "5 Whys Analysis," ToolsHero.com, 2012, https://www.toolshero.com/problem-solving/5-whys-analysis/.
5. Julia Burdick-Will, Marc L. Stein, and Jeffrey Grigg, "Danger on the Way to School: Exposure to Violent Crime, Public Transportation, and Absenteeism," *Sociological Science* 6 (2019): 118–42, doi:10.15195/v6.a5.
6. Marc L. Stein and Jeffrey A. Grigg, "Missing Bus, Missing School: Establishing the Relationship Between Public Transit Use and Student Absenteeism," *American Educational Research Journal* 56, no. 5 (2019): 1834–60, doi:10.3102/0002831219833917; Marc L. Stein et al., *Getting to High School in Baltimore: Student Commuting and Public Transportation* (Baltimore: Baltimore Education Research Consortium, 2017), http://baltimore-berc.org/wp-content/uploads/2017/01/GettingtoHighSchoolinBaltimoreJanuary2017.pdf.
7. This map only addresses one part of the system. One can develop similar ones for the classroom instruction and other key areas.
8. Donald B. Ardell, *High Level Wellness: An Alternative to Doctors, Drugs, and Disease* (Berkeley, CA: Ten Speed Press, 1986), cited in Larry Cohen and Sana

Chehimi, "Beyond Brochures: The Imperative for Primary Prevention," in *Prevention Is Primary: Strategies for Community Wellbeing*, ed. Larry Cohen, Vivian Chávez, and Sana Chehimi (Oakland, CA: Prevention Institute, 2007), 4–5.

9. See, for example, Elaine Allensworth and John Q. Easton, *What Matters for Staying On-Track and Graduating in Chicago Public Schools: A Close Look at Course Grades, Failures, and Attendance in the Freshman Year* (Chicago: Consortium on Chicago School Research, 2007), https://consortium.uchicago.edu/publications/what-matters-staying-track-and-graduating-chicago-public-schools; and Robert Balfanz, Liza Herzog, and Douglas J. Mac Iver, "Preventing Student Disengagement and Keeping Students on the Graduation Path in Urban Middle-Grades Schools: Early Identification and Effective Interventions," *Educational Psychologist* 42, no. 4 (2007): 223–35, doi:10.1080/00461520701621079.
10. Jessica B. Heppen and Susan Bowles Therriault, *Developing Early Warning Systems to Identify Potential High School Dropouts* (Washington, DC: National High School Center, 2008), https://files.eric.ed.gov/fulltext/ED521558.pdf; Craig D. Jerald, *Identifying Potential Dropouts: Key Lessons for Building an Early Warning Data System* (Washington, DC: Achieve, Inc., 2006), https://www.achieve.org/publications/identifying-potential-dropouts-key-lessons-building-early-warning-data-system; Louise Kennelley and Maggie Monrad, *Approaches to Dropout Prevention: Heeding Early Warning Signs with Appropriate Interventions* (Washington, DC: National High School Center, 2007), https://files.eric.ed.gov/fulltext/ED499009.pdf; Lyndsay Pinkus, *Using Early-Warning Data to Improve Graduation Rates: Closing Cracks in the Education System* (Washington, DC: Alliance for Excellent Education, 2008), https://all4ed.org/wp-content/uploads/EWI.pdf; and Susan Bowles Therriault et al., *High School Early Warning Intervention Monitoring System Implementation Guide* (Washington, DC: National High School Center, 2013), https://www.air.org/sites/default/files/High-School-Early-Warning-Intervention-Implementation-Guide-March-2013.pdf.
11. *Issue Brief: Early Warning Systems* (Washington, DC: US Department of Education, 2016), https://www2.ed.gov/rschstat/eval/high-school/early-warning-systems-brief.pdf.
12. Ann-Marie Faria et al., *Getting Students On Track for Graduation: Impacts of the Early Warning Intervention and Monitoring System After One Year* (Washington, DC: US Department of Education, Institute of Education Sciences, National Center for Education Evaluation and Regional Assistance, Regional Educational Laboratory Midwest, 2017), http://ies.ed.gov/ncee/edlabs/projects/project.asp?projectID=388; Martha Abele Mac Iver et al., "An Efficacy Study of a Ninth-Grade Early Warning Indicator Intervention," *Journal of Research on Educational Effectiveness* 12, no. 3 (2019): 363–90, doi:10.1080/19345747.2019.1615156; and Trisha Borman et al., *I3 BARR Validation Study Impact Findings: Cohorts 1 and 2* (Washington, DC: American Institutes for Research, 2018), https://www.air.org/sites/default/files/BARR-report-cohorts-1-and-2-December-2018-rev.pdf.
13. *Issue Brief: Early Warning Systems.*
14. Attendance Works and the Everyone Graduates Center, *Using Chronic Absence To Map Interrupted Schooling, Instructional Loss, and Educational Inequity:*

Insights from School Year 2017–18 Data (Baltimore: Attendance Works and Johns Hopkins University, February 2021), https://www.attendanceworks.org/wp-content/uploads/2019/06/Attendance-Works-Using-Chronic-Absence-to-Map_020221.pdf.

15. Linda S. Olsen, *Why September Matters: Improving Student Attendance* (Baltimore: Baltimore Education Research Consortium, 2014), https://eric.ed.gov/?id=ED553161.
16. Mindee O'Cummings et al., *Early Warning System High School Tool Technical Manual* (Washington, DC: National High School Center, 2010).
17. See, for example, William H. Jeynes, "The Relationship Between Parental Involvement and Urban Secondary School Student Academic Achievement: A Meta-Analysis," *Urban Education* 42, no. 1 (January 2007): 82–110, doi:10.1177/0042085906293818.
18. Steven B. Sheldon, "Improving Student Attendance with School, Family, and Community Partnerships," *The Journal of Educational Research* 100, no. 5 (2007): 267–75, doi:10.3200/JOER.100.5.267-275; Joyce L. Epstein and Steven B. Sheldon, "Present and Accounted For: Improving Student Attendance Through Family and Community Involvement," *The Journal of Educational Research* 95, no. 5 (2002): 308–18, doi:10.1080/00220670209596604; and Steven B. Sheldon and Joyce L. Epstein, "Getting Students to School: Using Family and Community Involvement to Reduce Chronic Absenteeism," *School Community Journal* 14, no. 2 (Fall/Winter 2004): 39–56.
19. Carly D. Robinson et al., "Reducing Student Absenteeism in the Early Grades by Targeting Parental Beliefs," *American Educational Research Journal* 55, no. 6 (December 2018): 1163–92, doi:10.3102/0002831218772274; Todd Rogers et al., *A Randomized Experiment Using Absenteeism Information to "Nudge" Attendance* (Washington, DC: US Department of Education, Institute of Education Sciences, National Center for Education Evaluation and Regional Assistance, Regional Educational Laboratory Mid-Atlantic, 2017), https://ies.ed.gov/ncee/edlabs/regions/midatlantic/pdf/REL_2017252.pdf; and Todd Rogers and Avi Feller, "Reducing Student Absences at Scale by Targeting Parents' Misbeliefs," *Nature Human Behaviour* 2 (2018): 335–42, doi:10.1038/s41562-018-0328-1.
20. Beth S. Simon, "High School Outreach and Family Involvement," *Social Psychology of Education* 7, no. 2 (June 2004): 185–209, doi:10.1023/B:SPOE.0000018559.47658.67.
21. Emily Krone Phillips, *The Make-or-Break Year: Solving the Dropout Crisis One Ninth Grader at a Time* (New York: The New Press, 2019); and Christopher Spera, "A Review of the Relationship Among Parenting Practices, Parenting Styles, and Adolescent School Achievement," *Educational Psychology Review* 17, no. 2 (June 2005): 125–46, doi:10.1007/s10648-005-3950-1.
22. Todd Rosenkranz et al., *Free to Fail or On-Track to College: Why Grades Drop When Students Enter High School and What Adults Can Do About It* (Chicago: University of Chicago Consortium on Chicago School Research, 2014), https://consortium.uchicago.edu/sites/default/files/2018-10/FoF%20Why%20Grades%20Drop.pdf; Melissa Roderick, "What's Happening to the Boys? Early High School Experiences and School Outcomes Among African American Male Adolescents in Chicago," *Urban Education* 38, no. 5 (2003):

538–607, doi:10.1177/0042085903256221; Brian K. Barber and Joseph A. Olsen, "Assessing the Transitions to Middle and High School," *Journal of Adolescent Research* 19, no. 1 (2004): 3–30, doi:10.1177/0743558403258113.

23. Joyce L. Epstein et al., *School, Family, and Community Partnerships: Your Handbook for Action*, fourth ed. (Thousand Oaks, CA: Corwin, 2018).
24. Centers for Disease Control and Prevention, *School Connectedness: Strategies for Increasing Protective Factors Among Youth* (Atlanta: US Department of Health and Human Services, 2009), https://www.cdc.gov/healthyyouth/protective/pdf/connectedness.pdf; and Terence Bowles and Janet Scull, "The Centrality of Connectedness: A Conceptual Synthesis of Attending, Belong, Engaging and Flowing," *Journal of Psychologists and Counsellors in Schools* 29, no. 1 (June 2019): 3–21, doi:10.1017/jgc.2018.13.
25. Clayton R. Cook et al., "Positive Greetings at the Door: Evaluation of a Low-Cost, High-Yield Proactive Classroom Management Strategy," *Journal of Positive Behavior Interventions* 20, no. 3 (July 2018): 149–59, doi:10.1177/1098300717753831.
26. See, for example, Clea A. McNeely, James M. Nonnemaker, and Robert W. Blum, "Promoting School Connectedness: Evidence from the National Longitudinal Study of Adolescent Health," *Journal of School Health* 72, no. 4 (April 2002): 138–46, doi:10.1111/j.1746-1561.2002.tb06533.x; and Tanya Forneris, Martin Camiré, and Robert Williamson, "Extracurricular Activity Participation and the Acquisition of Developmental Assets: Differences Between Involved and Noninvolved Canadian High School Students," *Applied Developmental Science* 19, no. 1 (2015): 47–55, doi:10.1080/10888691.2014.980580.
27. See, for example, Susana Claro and Susanna Loeb, "Self-Management Skills and Student Achievement Gains: Evidence from California's CORE Districts" (working paper, Policy Analysis for California Education, Stanford, CA, September 2019), https://edpolicyinca.org/publications/self-management-skills-and-student-achievement-gains-evidence-california-core-districts; and Camille Farrington et al., *Teaching Adolescents to Become Learners. The Role of Noncognitive Factors in Shaping School Performance: A Critical Literature Review* (Chicago: University of Chicago Consortium on Chicago School Research, 2012), https://consortium.uchicago.edu/publications/teaching-adolescents-become-learners-role-noncognitive-factors-shaping-school.
28. See, for example, Clive Belfield et al., *The Economic Value of Social and Emotional Learning* (New York: Center for Benefit-Cost Studies in Education, 2015), http://www.casel.org/wp-content/uploads/2016/09/SEL-Revised.pdf; James J. Heckman, Jora Stixrud, and Sergio Urzua, "The Effects of Cognitive and Noncognitive Abilities on Labor Market Outcomes and Social Behavior," *Journal of Labor Economics* 24, no. 3 (July 2006): 411–82, doi:10.1086/504455; and Erik Lindqvist and Roine Vestman, "The Labor Market Returns to Cognitive and Noncognitive Ability: Evidence from the Swedish Enlistment," *American Economic Journal: Applied Economics* 3, no. 1 (January 2011): 101–28, doi:10.1257/app.3.1.101.
29. Elaine Allensworth et al., *Looking Forward to High School and College: Middle Grade Indicators of Readiness in Chicago Public Schools* (Chicago: University of Chicago Consortium on Chicago School Research, 2014), https://

consortium.uchicago.edu/publications/looking-forward-high-school-and-college-middle-grade-indicators-readiness-chicago.

30. Martin R. West et al., "Trends in Student Social-Emotional Learning: Evidence from the First Large-Scale Panel Student Survey," *Educational Evaluation and Policy Analysis* 42, no. 2 (June 2020): 279–303, doi:10.3102/0162373720912236.
31. Camille Farrington, Shanette Porter, and Joshua Klugman, "Do Classroom Environments Matter for Noncognitive Aspects of Student Performance and Students' Course Grades?" (working paper, UChicago Consortium on School Research, 2019), https://consortium.uchicago.edu/publications/do-classroom-environments-matter-for-noncognitive-aspects-of-student-performance-and-students-course-grades; and David S. Yeager and Gregory M. Walton, "Social-Psychological Interventions in Education: They're Not Magic," *Review of Educational Research* 81, no. 2 (June 2011): 267–301, doi:10.3102/0034654311405999.
32. Aspen Institute, *From a Nation at Risk to a Nation at Hope: Recommendations from the National Commission on Social, Emotional, & Academic Development* (Washington, DC: Aspen Institute, 2019), http://nationathope.org/report-from-the-nation/; and Mary Helen Immordino-Yang, Linda Darling-Hammond, and Christina Krone, *The Brain Basis for Integrated Social, Emotional, and Academic Development: How Emotions and Social Relationships Drive Learning* (Washington, DC: Aspen Institute, 2018), https://www.aspeninstitute.org/publications/the-brain-basis-for-integrated-social-emotional-and-academic-development/.
33. David S. Yeager et al., "Using Design Thinking to Improve Psychological Interventions: The Case of the Growth Mindset During the Transition to High School," *Journal of Educational Psychology* 108, no. 3 (2016): 374–91, doi:10.1037/edu0000098; David S. Yeager, "Social and Emotional Learning Programs for Adolescents," *The Future of Children* 27, no. 1 (Spring 2017): 73–94, https://www.jstor.org/stable/44219022; C. Lee Williams et al., "A Brief Social Belonging Intervention Improves Academic Outcomes for Minoritized High School Students," *Motivation Science* 6, no. 4 (2020): 423–37, doi:10.1037/mot0000175; and Susan Headden and Susan McKay, *Motivation Matters: How New Research Can Help Teachers Boost Student Engagement* (Stanford, CA: Carnegie Foundation for the Advancement of Teaching, 2015), https://www.carnegiefoundation.org/wp-content/uploads/2015/07/Motivation_Matters_July_2015.pdf.
34. West et al., "Trends in Student Social-Emotional Learning."
35. Heather C. Hill et al., "Teacher Quality and Quality Teaching: Examining the Relationship of a Teacher Assessment to Practice," *American Journal of Education* 118, no. 4 (August 2012): 489–519, doi:10.1086/666380; Heather C. Hill et al., "Mathematical Knowledge for Teaching and the Mathematical Quality of Instruction: An Exploratory Study," *Cognition and Instruction* 26, no. 4 (2008): 430–511, doi:10.1080/07370000802177235; and *A Closer Look at the Five Essential Components of Effective Reading Instruction: A Review of Scientifically Based Reading Research for Teachers* (Naperville, IL: Learning Point Associates, 2004), https://files.eric.ed.gov/fulltext/ED512569.pdf.

36. Tuan Dinh Nguyen, Marisa Cannata, and Jason Miller, "Understanding Student Behavioral Engagement: Importance of Student Interaction with Peers and Teachers," *The Journal of Educational Research* 111, no. 2 (2018): 163–74, doi:10.1080/00220671.2016.1220359; Daniel Quin, "Longitudinal and Contextual Associations between Teacher-Student Relationships and Student Engagement: A Systematic Review," *Review of Educational Research* 87, no. 2 (April 2017): 345–87, doi:10.3102/0034654316669434; and Debora L. Roorda et al., "The Influence of Affective Teacher-Student Relationships on Students' School Engagement and Achievement: A Meta-Analytic Approach," *Review of Educational Research* 81, no. 4 (December 2011): 493–529, doi:10.3102/0034654311421793.
37. Valerie E. Lee et al., *Social Support, Academic Press, and Student Achievement: A View from the Middle Grades in Chicago* (Chicago: Chicago Annenberg Research Project, 1999), https://consortium.uchicago.edu/publications/social-support-academic-press-and-student-achievement-view-middle-grades-chicago; and Ronald F. Ferguson et al., *The Influence of Teaching Beyond Standardized Test Scores: Engagement, Mindsets, and Agency* (Cambridge, MA: Harvard University Achievement Gap Initiative, 2015), http://www.agi.harvard.edu/projects/TeachingandAgency.pdf.
38. Lynley H. Anderman and Valerie S. Leake, "The ABCs of Motivation: An Alternative Framework for Teaching Preservice Teachers about Motivation," *The Clearing House* 78, no. 5 (May–June 2005): 192–96, https://www.jstor.org/stable/30189907; Laura L. Pendergast and Avi Kaplan, "Instructional Context and Student Motivation, Learning, and Development: Commentary and Implications for School Psychologists," *School Psychology International* 36, no. 6 (December 2015): 638–47, doi:10.1177/0143034315613560; and Erik A. Ruzek et al., "How Teacher Emotional Support Motivates Students: The Mediating Roles of Perceived Peer Relatedness, Autonomy Support, and Competence," *Learning and Instruction* 42 (April 2016): 95–103, doi:10.1016/j.learninstruc.2016.01.004.
39. Chris S. Hulleman and Judith M. Harackiewicz, "Promoting Interest and Performance in High School Science Classes," *Science* 326 (December 4, 2009): 1410–12, doi:10.1126/science.1177067; and Karen Mitchell et al., *Rigor, Relevance, and Results: The Quality of Teacher Assignments and Student Work in New and Conventional High Schools* (Washington, DC: American Institutes for Research and SRI International, 2005), https://www.air.org/sites/default/files/downloads/report/Rigor_Rpt_10_21_2005_0.pdf.
40. Barbara Condliffe et al., "Project-Based Learning: A Literature Review" (working paper, MDRC, New York, 2017), https://www.mdrc.org/publication/project-based-learning; and Douglas J. Mac Iver and Tristan M. Z. Hann, "Effective School Reforms for Increasing Engagement," in *Handbook of Student Engagement Interventions: Working with Disengaged Students*, ed. Jennifer A. Fredricks, Amy L. Reschly, and Sandra L. Christenson (San Diego, CA: Academic Press, 2019), 245–61, doi:10.1016/B978-0-12-813413-9.00017-6.
41. Aleidine J. Moeller, Janine M. Theiler, and Chaorong Wu, "Goal Setting and Student Achievement: A Longitudinal Study," *Modern Language Journal* 96, no. 2 (Summer 2012): 153–69, doi:10.1111/j.1540-4781.2011.01231.x; and Pendergast and Kaplan, "Instructional Context."

Chapter 4

1. Anthony S. Bryk et al., *Learning to Improve: How America's Schools Can Get Better at Getting Better* (Cambridge, MA: Harvard Education Press, 2015), 87.
2. Anthony S. Bryk, *Improvement in Action: Advancing Quality in America's Schools* (Cambridge, MA: Harvard Education Press, 2020), 140.
3. *NCSSFL-ACTFL Can-Do Statements: Progress Indicators for Language Learners* (Alexandria, VA: ACTFL, 2015), http://ujop.cuni.cz/upload/stories/Sluzby/Can-Do_Statements.pdf.
4. *Measures that Matter Most: How Do Next Generation Educators Measure Success?* (San Francisco: Next Generation Learning Challenges, 2016), https://www.nextgenlearning.org/resources/measures-that-matter-most-research-report.
5. "Critical Thinking & Problem Solving," Learn with Two Rivers, https://www.learnwithtworivers.org/critical-thinking--problem-solving.html.
6. "Summit Public Schools—Habits of Success Assessment," Next Generation Learning Challenges, https://www.nextgenlearning.org/grantee/summit-public-schools-1; "Summit Public Schools—Habits of Success Assessment Artifact April 2016," https://drive.google.com/file/d/0B5mcyFEu5BpnX29 xSzNo MlZOdlU/view.
7. Robert Balfanz and Vaughn Byrnes, *Connecting Social-Emotional Development, Academic Achievement, and On-Track Outcomes: A Multi-District Study of Grades 3 to 10 Students Supported by City Year AmeriCorps Members* (Baltimore: Everyone Graduates Center, Johns Hopkins University School of Education, 2020), http://new.every1graduates.org/wp-content/uploads/2020/05/201200507_EGC_CityYearReport_BalfanzByrnesFINAL.pdf. The DESSA is based on eight items, covering personal responsibility, optimistic thinking, goal-directed behavior, social awareness, decision-making, relationship skills, self-awareness, and self-management. See Jack A. Naglieri, Paul LeBuffe, and Valerie B. Shapiro, "Universal Screening for Social-Emotional Competencies: A Study of the Reliability and Validity of the DESSA-mini," *Psychology in the Schools* 48, no. 7 (August 2011): 660–71, doi:10.1002/pits.20586.
8. Bryk et al., *Learning to Improve*, 46.
9. See, for example, our flowchart of the process steps involved in getting parents connected to the parent portal in Martha Abele Mac Iver, Steven Sheldon, and Emily Clark, "Widening the Portal: How Schools Can Help More Families Access and Use the Parent Portal to Support Student Success," *Middle School Journal* 52, no. 1 (January 2021): 14–22, doi:10.1080/00940771.2020.1840269.
10. Megan Kuhfeld, "When Students Grade Their Teachers: A Validity Analysis of the Tripod Student Survey," *Educational Assessment* 22, no. 4 (2017): 253–74, doi:10.1080/10627197.2017.1381555; and Ronald F. Ferguson, "Can Student Surveys Measure Teaching Quality?" *Phi Delta Kappan* 94, no. 3 (November 2012): 24–28, doi:10.1177/003172171209400306.
11. See PERTS, https://www.perts.net/elevate. The link to the survey on this page takes the reader to https://docs.google.com/document/d/1NbRmslY905tVWRIC0_iOYnPe-s0y3qeVlRgjFRglfWY/edit.
12. "Copilot-Elevate," PERTS, https://www.perts.net/elevate.

13. "Improvement Measures," CORE Districts, https://coredistricts.org/our-improvement-data/improvement-measures/.
14. When schools conduct their own improvement-focused surveys, they do not tend to encounter the same Institutional Review Board requirements for active parental consent that external researchers sometimes encounter when seeking to conduct similar work.
15. For background on family survey response rates, see Greg Austin, "Using a Parent Survey to Improve Parent Involvement and School Climate" (paper presented at the Office of Safe and Drug-Free Schools National Conference, Washington, DC, August 10, 2011); and Lori Nathanson, Meghan McCormick, and James J. Kemple, *Strengthening Assessments of School Climate: Lessons from the NYC School Survey* (New York: The Research Alliance for New York City Schools, 2013), https://research.steinhardt.nyu.edu/research_alliance/publications/nyc_school_survey.
16. See, for example, Sola Takahashi, "Revisiting the Purposes of Practical Measurement for Improvement: Learning from the BTEN Measurement System," *Carnegie Commons Blog*, August 21, 2014, https://www.carnegiefoundation.org/blog/revisiting-purposes-practical-measurement-improvement-learning-bten-measurement-system/.

Chapter 5

1. Anthony S. Bryk et al., *Learning to Improve: How America's Schools Can Get Better at Getting Better* (Cambridge, MA: Harvard Education Press, 2015), 114.
2. *Issue Brief: Early Warning Systems* (Washington, DC: US Department of Education, 2016), https://www2.ed.gov/rschstat/eval/high-school/early-warning-systems-brief.pdf.
3. See, for example, Ann-Marie Faria et al., *Getting Students On Track for Graduation: Impacts of the Early Warning Intervention and Monitoring System After One Year* (Washington, DC: US Department of Education, Institute of Education Sciences, National Center for Education Evaluation and Regional Assistance, Regional Educational Laboratory Midwest, 2017), http://ies.ed.gov/ncee/edlabs/projects/project.asp?projectID=388; and Martha Abele Mac Iver et al., "An Efficacy Study of a Ninth-Grade Early Warning Indicator Intervention," *Journal of Research on Educational Effectiveness* 12, no. 3 (2019): 363–90, doi:10.1080/19345747.2019.1615156.
4. Ruth Curran Neild, Robert Balfanz, and Liza Herzog, "An Early Warning System," *Educational Leadership* 65, no. 2 (October 2007): 28–33, http://www.ascd.org/publications/educational-leadership/oct07/vol65/num02/An-Early-Warning-System.aspx.
5. Peter Bergman, *Technology Adoption in Education: Usage, Spillovers and Student Achievement,* CESifo Working Paper No. 6101 (Munich: Ludwig Maximilians University Center for Economic Studies & Ifo Institute, 2016), https://www.cesifo.org/en/publikationen/2016/working-paper/technology-adoption-education-usage-spillovers-and-student; Peter Bergman, "Nudging Technology Use: Descriptive and Experimental Evidence from School Information Systems," *Education Finance and Policy* 15, no. 4 (2020): 623–47, doi:10.1162/edfp_a_00291; and Martha Abele Mac Iver et al., "Urban Parents at the

Portal: Family Use of Web-Based Information on Student Course Grades," *School Community Journal* (forthcoming 2021).

6. See, for example, Bergman, "Nudging Technology Use."
7. One of our colleagues who studies family engagement, Steven Sheldon, has shared with us his own positive experience with receiving regular text messages from teachers about upcoming assignments for his middle school child.
8. Peter Bergman, "Parent-Child Information Frictions and Human Capital Investment: Evidence from a Field Experiment," *Journal of Political Economy* (forthcoming), http://www.columbia.edu/~psb2101/BergmanSubmission.pdf.
9. Clayton R. Cook et al., "Positive Greetings at the Door: Evaluation of a Low-Cost, High-Yield Proactive Classroom Management Strategy," *Journal of Positive Behavior Interventions* 20, no. 3 (July 2018): 149–59, doi:10.1177/1098300717753831.
10. Cook et al., "Positive Greetings."
11. Cook et al., "Positive Greetings," 151.
12. "Copilot-Elevate," PERTS, https://www.perts.net/elevate.
13. For evidence on "check and connect," see Mary F. Sinclair et al., "Facilitating Student Engagement: Lessons Learned from Check & Connect Longitudinal Studies," *The California School Psychologist* 8, no. 1 (January 2003): 29–41, doi:10.1007/BF03340894.
14. David Paunesku et al., "Mind-Set Interventions Are a Scalable Treatment for Academic Underachievement," *Psychological Science* 26, no. 6 (June 1, 2015): 784–93, doi:10.1177/0956797615571017; and David S. Yeager et al., "Boring but Important: A Self-Transcendent Purpose for Learning Fosters Academic Self-Regulation," *Journal of Personality and Social Psychology* 107, no. 4 (October 2014): 559–80, doi:10.1037/a0037637.
15. See discussion of the Summit Schools experience in Anthony S. Bryk, *Improvement in Action: Advancing Quality in America's Schools* (Cambridge, MA: Harvard Education Press, 2020), 89–90.
16. Carol S. Dweck, *Mindset: The New Psychology of Success* (New York: Random House Digital, Inc., 2008).
17. David S. Yeager et al., "A National Experiment Reveals Where a Growth Mindset Improves Achievement," *Nature* 573 (September 19, 2019): 364–69, doi:10.1038/s41586-019-1466-y; David S. Yeager et al., "Using Design Thinking to Improve Psychological Interventions: The Case of the Growth Mindset During the Transition to High School," *Journal of Educational Psychology* 108, no. 3 (April 2016): 374–91, doi:10.1037/edu0000098.
18. See the PERTS Growth Mindset for 9th Graders page and downloadable information packet, https://www.perts.net/orientation/hg.
19. See the PERTS Growth Mindset for 9th Graders page cited above.
20. Yeager et al., "Using Design Thinking."
21. See Fiona S. Seaton, "Empowering Teachers to Implement a Growth Mindset," *Educational Psychology in Practice* 34, no. 1 (2018): 41–57, doi:10.1080/02667363.2017.1382333.
22. David S. Yeager and Matthew Bundick, "The Role of Purposeful Work Goals in Promoting Meaning in Life and in Schoolwork During Adolescence," *Journal of Adolescent Research* 24, no. 4 (July 1, 2009): 423–52,

doi:10.1177/0743558409336749; and Paunesku et al., "Mind-Set Interventions."

23. For more details about the way the research team designed the intervention, see Yeager et al., "Boring but Important."
24. The quote read to students was: "For me, getting an education is all about learning things that will help me do something I can feel good about, something that matters for the world. I used to do my schoolwork just to earn a better grade and look smart. I still think doing well in school is important, but for me it's definitely not just about a grade anymore. I'm growing up, and doing well in school is all about preparing myself to do something that matters, something that I care about." The writing prompt was: *How could the world be a better place? Sometimes the world isn't fair, and so everyone thinks it could be better in one way or another. Some people want there to be less hunger, some want less prejudice, and others want less violence or disease. Other people want lots of* other *changes. What are some ways that you think the world could be a better place?* Yeager et al., "Boring but Important," 568.
25. See www.perts.net/elevate for the survey measures about "meaningful work."
26. See, for example, Johnny B. Allred and Michael E. Cena, "Reading Motivation in High School: Instructional Shifts in Student Choice and Class Time," *Journal of Adolescent & Adult Literacy* 64, no.1 (July/August 2020): 27–35, doi:10.1002/jaal.1058.
27. Allred and Cena, "Reading Motivation in High School"; Frédéric Guay, Catherine F. Ratelle, and Julien Chanal, "Optimal Learning in Optimal Contexts: The Role of Self-Determination in Education," *Canadian Psychology* 49, no. 3 (2008): 233–40, doi:10.1037/a0012758; and Johnmarshall Reeve et al., "Enhancing Students' Engagement by Increasing Teachers' Autonomy Support," *Motivation and Emotion* 28, no. 2 (June 2004): 147–69, doi:10.1023/B:MOEM.0000032312.95499.6f.
28. See "Authentic Assessment Ideas" posted under "Assessment that Motivates," Everyone Graduates Center, https://www.engage.every1graduates.org/teacher-resources/.
29. Aleidine J. Moeller, Janine M. Theiler, and Chaorong Wu, "Goal Setting and Student Achievement: A Longitudinal Study," *Modern Language Journal* 96, no. 2 (Summer 2012): 153–69, doi:10.1111/j.1540-4781.2011.01231.x.
30. Matt Townsley, "Redesigning Grading—Districtwide," *Educational Leadership* 71, no. 4 (December 2013/January 2014): 68–71, http://www.ascd.org/publications/educational-leadership/dec13/vol71/num04/Redesigning-Grading%E2%80%94Districtwide.aspx.
31. This quote from a fellow teacher, reported in Myron Dueck, *Grading Smarter, Not Harder: Assessment Strategies That Motivate Kids and Help Them Learn* (Alexandria, VA: ASCD, 2014), 93, was echoed by a teacher in one of our professional development series, who cited the O-rings in the *Challenger* disaster for evidence. As Myron Dueck points out, however, there are very few times in the real world when you get just one chance to demonstrate your knowledge. Almost all situations in life provide opportunities for some kind of retest or second chance. The issue is whether or not we label people as failures between the chances.

32. Myron Dueck addresses this issue as well in *Grading Smarter, Not Harder*, 90–117.
33. See unit plans and progress monitoring tools posted under "Assessment that Motivates," Everyone Graduates Center, https://www.engage.every1graduates.org/teacher-resources/.
34. Barbara Condliffe et al., "Project-Based Learning: A Literature Review" (working paper, MDRC, New York, 2017), https://www.mdrc.org/publication/project-based-learning. Also see Douglas J. Mac Iver and Tristan M. Z. Hann, "Effective School Reforms for Increasing Engagement," in *Handbook of Student Interventions: Working with Disengaged Students*, ed. Jennifer A. Fredricks, Amy L. Reschly, and Sandra L. Christenson (San Diego, CA: Academic Press, 2019), 245–61, doi:10.1016/B978-0-12-813413-9.00017-6.
35. Condliffe et al., "Project-Based Learning," 52.
36. See the extensive library of PBL resources on the Buck Institute for Education's PBLWorks website: https://www.pblworks.org/.
37. Martha Abele Mac Iver and Douglas J. Mac Iver, "'STEMming' the Swell of Absenteeism in the Middle Years: Impacts of an Urban District Summer Robotics Program," *Urban Education* 54, no. 1 (January 1, 2019): 65–88, doi:10.1177/0042085915618712; and Martha Abele Mac Iver and Douglas J. Mac Iver, *The Baltimore City Schools Middle School STEM Summer Program with VEX Robotics* (Baltimore: Baltimore Education Research Consortium, 2015), https://files.eric.ed.gov/fulltext/ED570654.pdf.
38. "Nagging and nurturing" was a favorite expression of the longtime director of our Center for Social Organization of Schools at Johns Hopkins University, James McPartland, who began the work of Talent Development High Schools in Baltimore in the mid-1990s.
39. See resources posted on https://www.hsredesign.org/getting-started/needs-assessments/.
40. Bryk et al., *Learning to Improve*, 141.

Chapter 6

1. Ralph T. Putnam and Hilda Borko, "What Do New Views of Knowledge and Thinking Have to Say About Research on Teacher Learning?," *Educational Researcher* 29, no. 1 (January 1, 2000): 4–15, doi:10.3102/0013189X029001004.
2. Also see Marisa Cannata, Lora Cohen-Vogel, and Michael Sorum, "Partnering for Improvement: Improvement Communities and Their Role in Scale Up," *Peabody Journal of Education* 92, no. 5 (2017): 569–88, doi:10.1080/0161956X.2017.1368633.
3. See, for example, Susana C. Marques, J. L. Pais-Ribeiro, and Shane J. Lopez, "The Role of Positive Psychology Constructs in Predicting Mental Health and Academic Achievement in Children and Adolescents: A Two-Year Longitudinal Study," *Journal of Happiness Studies* 12, no. 6 (December 2011): 1049–62, doi:10.1007/s10902-010-9244-4; and Susana C. Marques, Matthew W. Gallagher, and Shane J. Lopez, "Hope- and Academic-Related Outcomes: A Meta-Analysis," *School Mental Health* 9, no. 3 (September 2017): 250–62, doi:10.1007/s12310-017-9212-9.
4. Policies that specify "no grades lower than 50" effectively transform the 100-point scale to one more like the 0 to 4 point scale. As we document elsewhere, however, such policies often generate considerable opposition because

giving students a 50 for unsubmitted work is perceived as getting something for nothing and encouraging a lack of responsibility. See Martha Abele Mac Iver, "When Minimum Grading Policies Backfire: Who Decides Whether to Let Students Fail?," in *When School Policies Backfire: How Well-Intended Measures Can Harm Our Most Vulnerable Students,* ed. Michael A. Gottfried and Gilberto Q. Conchas (Cambridge, MA: Harvard Education Press, 2016), 69–84.

5. Robert Balfanz et al., *Great American High School Campaign: Reforming the Nation's Remaining Low-Performing High Schools* (Washington, DC, and Baltimore: Civic Enterprises and Everyone Graduates Center, Johns Hopkins University, 2018), 2, https://www.americaspromise.org/sites/default/files/d8/GreatAmericanHighSchoolCampaignReport.pdf.
6. Miriam Komaromy et al., "Project ECHO (Extension for Community Healthcare Outcomes): A New Model for Educating Primary Care Providers About Treatment of Substance Use Disorders," *Substance Abuse* 37, no. 1 (2016): 20–24, doi:10.1080/08897077.2015.1129388.
7. Martha Abele Mac Iver et al., "Engaging Families in the High School Transition: Initial Findings from a Continuous Improvement Initiative," *School Community Journal* 28, no. 1 (2018): 37–66, https://files.eric.ed.gov/fulltext/EJ1184768.pdf.
8. Martha Abele Mac Iver, Steven Sheldon, and Emily Clark, "Widening the Portal: How Schools Can Help More Families Access and Use the Parent Portal to Support Student Success," *Middle School Journal* 52, no. 1 (January 2021): 14–22, doi:10.1080/00940771.2020.1840269.
9. See, for example, Susan Enfield and Alan Spicciati, "Reculturing the Central Office," *School Administrator* 71, no. 4 (April 2014): 27–30, https://www.aasa.org/content.aspx?id=32746; and Meredith I. Honig and Lydia R. Rainey, "Central Office Leadership in Principal Professional Learning Communities: The Practice Beneath the Policy," *Teachers College Record* 116, no. 4 (2014): 1–48, http://www.tcrecord.org/Content.asp?ContentId=17404. While the continuous improvement work of the National Center on Scaling Up Effective Schools involved central office administrators as well as high school faculty members on their design teams, the continuous improvement training and collaborative meetings were led by researchers rather than by the district office staff. See Ariel Tichnor-Wagner et al., "Continuous Improvement in the Public School Context: Understanding How Educators Respond to Plan–Do–Study–Act Cycles," *Journal of Educational Change* 18, no. 4 (November 2017): 465–94, doi:10.1007/s10833-017-9301-4.
10. Anthony S. Bryk, *Improvement in Action: Advancing Quality in America's Schools* (Cambridge, MA: Harvard Education Press, 2020), Chapter 7.
11. Bryk, *Improvement in Action,* Chapter 6.
12. Contact Martha Mac Iver at mmaciver@jhu.edu and Robert Balfanz at rbalfanz@jhu.edu.
13. See, for example, the Minnesota Department of Education webpage on continuous improvement resources, https://education.mn.gov/MDE/dse/cimp/.

Chapter 7

1. Emma García and Elaine Weiss, *COVID-19 and Student Performance, Equity, and U.S. Education Policy: Lessons from Pre-Pandemic Research to Inform Relief, Recovery, and Rebuilding* (Washington DC: Economic Policy Institute,

September 10, 2020), https://www.epi.org/publication/the-consequences-of-the-covid-19-pandemic-for-education-performance-and-equity-in-the-united-states-what-can-we-learn-from-pre-pandemic-research-to-inform-relief-recovery-and-rebuilding/; and Andreas Schleicher, *The Impact of COVID-19 on Education: Insights from* Education at a Glance 2020 (Paris: OECD, 2020), https://www.oecd.org/education/the-impact-of-covid-19-on-education-insights-education-at-a-glance-2020.pdf.

2. Valerie Strauss, "More Students Than Ever Got F's in First Term of 2020-21 School Year—But Are A-F Grades Fair in a Pandemic?," *Washington Post*, December 6, 2020, https://www.washingtonpost.com/education/2020/12/06/more-students-than-ever-got-fs-first-term-2020-21-school-year-are-a-f-grades-fair-pandemic/ (the article cites data from five different states); and Madeline St. Amour, "Enrollment Still Down," *Inside Higher Ed*, November 12, 2020, https://www.insidehighered.com/news/2020/11/12/enrollment-declines-continue-national-student-clearinghouse-finds.
3. Zoë Kirsch, "When Siblings Become Teachers: It's Not Just Parents Who Find Themselves Thrust into the Demanding Role of At-Home Educators," *The 74 Million*, April 10, 2020, https://www.the74million.org/article/when-siblings-become-teachers-its-not-just-parents-who-find-themselves-thrust-into-the-demanding-role-of-at-home-educators/.
4. Joseph Trawick-Smith and Karen Hawley Miles, *Uncharted Waters: How a Whole-System Approach to Continuous Improvement Can Help Districts Chart a Course to Equity and Excellence This Pandemic School Year* (Watertown, MA: Education Resource Strategies, October 2020), https://www.erstrategies.org/tap/uncharted_waters.
5. Emiliana Vegas and Rebecca Winthrop, *Beyond Reopening Schools: How Education Can Reemerge Stronger Than Before COVID-19* (Washington, DC: Brookings Institution, 2020), https://www.brookings.edu/research/beyond-reopening-schools-how-education-can-emerge-stronger-than-before-covid-19/; and Fernando M. Reimers and Andreas Schleicher, *Schooling Disrupted, Schooling Rethought: How the Covid-19 Pandemic Is Changing Education* (Paris: OECD, 2020), 7, https://globaled.gse.harvard.edu/files/geii/files/education_continuity_v3.pdf.
6. Vegas and Winthrop, *Beyond Reopening Schools.*
7. Molly M. Scott, "Making High School More Flexible and Supportive for Teens After COVID-19," *Urban Wire: Education and Training* (blog), June 18, 2020, https://www.urban.org/urban-wire/making-high-school-more-flexible-and-supportive-teens-after-covid-19.
8. The district websites we view regularly have increased their family survey frequency and listening sessions dramatically. Some even post reports of survey results. See, for example, Paige DeBaylo, Karen Looby, and Holly Williams, *AISD Middle and High School Family Learning Preference Survey Results: October 2020* (Austin, TX: Austin Independent School District, 2020), https://www.austinisd.org/sites/default/files/dre-reports/OctoberLearningPreferenceSurvey_FinalResults_3.pdf; and Chad Getston, "Getston: My Arizona School District Contacts Every Student, Every Day, to Check on Families' Physical, Mental & Emotional Health. Yours Can, Too," *The 74 Million*, April 8, 2020, https://www.the74million.org/article/gestson-my-arizona-school-district

-contacts-every-student-every-day-to-check-on-families-physical-mental-emotional-health-yours-can-too/.

Grassroots efforts, such as "Just Ask Us" are actively seeking to hear and amplify the voices of students and families about what they "want from their schools in a time of social and economic crisis," www.justaskusmovement.org.

9. See https://www.nobodyaskedmebmore.org.
10. Anthony S. Bryk, *Improvement in Action: Advancing Quality in America's Schools* (Cambridge, MA: Harvard Education Press, 2020), 205.
11. See https://diplomasnow.org; https://ncs.uchicago.edu/; https://www.ctrise.org; https://www.newvisions.org; and https://barrcenter.org.
12. Sara Ray Stoelinga discusses these pendulum swings in the Critical Issues in Urban Education Coursera course from the University of Chicago, https://www.coursera.org/learn/urban-education.
13. Contact us at mmaciver@jhu.edu and rbalfanz@jhu.edu.

Appendix

1. See https://www.perts.net/elevate under "Elevate Student Voice" and "survey."
2. Sharon E. Paulsen, "Relations of Parenting Style and Parental Involvement with Ninth-Grade Students' Achievement," *Journal of Early Adolescence* 14, no. 2 (May 1, 1994): 250–67, doi:10.1177/027243169401400208.
3. Erik A. Ruzek et al., "How Teacher Emotional Support Motivates Students: The Mediating Roles of Perceived Peer Relatedness, Autonomy Support, and Competence," *Learning and Instruction* 42 (April 2016): 95–103, doi:10.1016/j.learninstruc.2016.01.004.
4. Corliss Bean, Meredith Rocchi, and Tanya Forneris, "Using the Learning Climate Questionnaire to Assess Basic Psychological Needs Support in Youth Sport," *Journal of Applied Sport Psychology* 32, no. 6 (2020): 585–606, doi:10.1080/10413200.2019.1571537. The Learning Climate Questionnaire comes from the work of Williams and colleagues: Geoffrey C. Williams et al., "Motivational Predictors of Weight Loss and Weight-Loss Maintenance," *Journal of Personality and Social Psychology* 70, no.1 (January 1996): 115–26, doi:10.1037//0022-3514.70.1.115.

Acknowledgments

We begin by thanking Caroline Chauncey, recently retired editor in chief of Harvard Education Press, for her role in bringing this book to publication. She invited a proposal for a somewhat different book, and during a long interactive process helped to cast the vision for what this book eventually became. Like every great teacher, she saw potential and called it forth, offering invaluable feedback and suggestions along the way. We cherish her gift of encouragement that propelled us through our own continuous improvement process.

We also thank our colleagues at the Center for Social Organization of Schools at Johns Hopkins University who have journeyed with us over the years in the work of transforming schools. Douglas Mac Iver has partnered with Martha in work and all other areas of life for four decades, and with Bob in the mission of CSOS since 1995. We thank James McPartland (now retired) and Joyce Epstein for their never-flagging leadership and encouragement in the work of improving schools. We are grateful for all we have learned from our other colleagues at Johns Hopkins as we have labored in the trenches together on many a project—Steven Sheldon, Eric Rice, Marcy Davis, Richard Lofton, Marc Stein, Rachel Durham (now at Notre Dame of Maryland University), Faith Connelly (now at McREL), Nettie Legters (now at Portland [OR] Public Schools), and Steve Plank (now at the Annie E. Casey Foundation). We honor the memory of Sam Stringfield, who taught us so much and left us too soon. Some of our deepest insights have come from working with the teachers and school leaders on our implementation team that has supported schools in adapting and using evidence-based tools and school improvement models across the nation. These include Maria Waltemeyer, Linda Muskauski, Thomas Acampora, Tara Madden, Doug Elmer, Cheree Davis, Matt Wernsdorfer, Maxine Wood, Jeffrey Robinson, Hannah Peria, Jeri Crispe, and Genevieve Hamer, among many others (including Leslie Jones, who left us too soon). We have also greatly benefited from learning together with our partners in the City Year School Design and Improvement Division: Ryan Mick, Paola Felix Encarnacion, Nate Kerr, and Stephanie Wu.

Those who attend to all the details in the publication process are worthy of particular acknowledgement. Emily Clark contributed many long hours to create figures, format endnotes, and navigate the editing process for this book, and we are deeply grateful for her cheerful labor, as well as for the help of Amanda Martorana. We also thank Jayne Fargnoli, editor in chief at Harvard Education Press, who together with Molly Grab shepherded this book in the final stages of publication.

Most importantly, we want to acknowledge the many students, teachers, and administrators who have fostered our learning as we have engaged with them in schools and districts over the years. They taught us the wisdom that is in the school and the classroom. We hope this book can contribute to improving the everyday experience of students in schools throughout our country by providing a set of tools and approaches that will enable that wisdom to be codified and spread.

This project was supported in part by the Bill and Melinda Gates Foundation (Networks for School Improvement) and by the Institute of Education Sciences, US Department of Education, through grant R305H150081 to the Johns Hopkins University. The opinions expressed are those of the authors and do not represent views of the Foundation, Institute, or the US Department of Education.

About the Authors

Martha Abele Mac Iver is an associate research professor in the School of Education at the Johns Hopkins University and affiliated with the Center for Social Organization of Schools and the Everyone Graduates Center. She is author (with Elizabeth Farley-Ripple) of *Bringing the District Back In* and of numerous journal articles. Since the mid-1990s she has conducted research and evaluation studies at all levels of the K–12 educational system, spending hundreds of hours observing classroom instruction and interviewing teachers, students, and administrators. She was one of the founding researchers of the Baltimore Education Research Consortium and held a senior urban research fellowship from the Council of the Great City Schools from 2009 to 2011 to study dropout predictors in Baltimore. Recent studies she has conducted include a randomized control trial evaluation of an early warning system intervention, development and evaluation of a professional development series for high school teachers, and a continuous improvement initiative around increasing schools' family engagement efforts during the transition to high school. She also serves as an associate editor for the *Journal of Education for Students Placed at Risk*. Prior to her education research career, she conducted public opinion research in Europe for the US government and taught political science at Occidental College. She holds a BA in European studies from Michigan State University and a PhD in political science from the University of Michigan.

Robert Balfanz is a research professor at the Center for Social Organization of Schools, Johns Hopkins University School of Education, and director of the Everyone Graduates Center. His work focuses on translating research findings into effective school improvement strategies and educational reforms. He publishes, conducts research, and leads technical assistance efforts on secondary school reform, improving high school graduation and college readiness rates, early warning systems, chronic absenteeism, social-emotional learning, and instructional improvements in high poverty schools. Currently he is leading the Cross State High School Redesign Collaborative with five states and seventy high schools, and the Pathways to Adult Success initiative with over 150 school districts, state departments of education, higher education institutions, and nonprofits. He was codirector of the National Student Attendance, Engagement, and Success Center and codeveloper of the Talent Development Secondary and Diplomas Now whole-school improvement models. His work was featured in PBS *Frontline*'s "The Education of Omarina," and he was awarded the Alliance for Excellent Education's Everyone a Graduate Award and the National Forum to Accelerate Middle-Grades Reform Joan Lipsitz Lifetime Achievement Award. In 2013 the Obama White House recognized him as a Champion for Change for African American education, and he has served as an education fellow for the G. W. Bush Institute. He has a BA from Johns Hopkins University and a PhD from the University of Chicago.

Index